Staffordshire Library and Information Service

Please return or renew or by the last date shown

If not required by other readers, this item may be renewed
in person, by post or telephone, online or by email.
To renew, either the book or ticket are required

24 Hour Renewal Line
0845 33 00 740

Staffordshire
County Council

THE ONLY WAY IS

ESSEX

Published by Century 2011

2 4 6 8 10 9 7 5 3 1

First published in Great Britain in 2011
by Century
Random House, 20 Vauxhall Bridge Road,
London SW1V 2SA

www.randomhouse.co.uk

Addresses for companies within The Random House Group Limited
can be found at: www.randomhouse.co.uk

The Random House Group Limited Reg. No. 954009

A CIP catalogue record for this book
is available from the British Library

ISBN 9781846059421

The Random House Group Limited supports The Forest Stewardship
Council (FSC), the leading international forest certification organisation.
All our titles that are printed on Greenpeace approved FSC certified paper carry the
FSC logo. Our paper procurement policy can be found at
www.rbooks.co.uk/environment

Printed and bound in Germany by
Firmengruppe APPL, aprinta Druck, Wemding

Design by www.envydesign.co.uk

THE ONLY WAY IS ESSEX

Official guide to living life the Essex way

ALEX HINES

CENTURY

CONTENTS

INTRO

> **Essex girl** *n. Brit. derogatory* a term applied (usu. *joc.*) to a type of young woman, supposedly to be found in and around Essex, and variously characterised as unintelligent, promiscuous, and materialistic

Oh yeah? Well, I'm sure that the lexicographer who wrote these definitions wouldn't be seen strutting his stuff down Loughton High Road, or mixing it up with the perfectly tanned and toned clientele of Sugar Hut or Nu Bar.

Well it's their loss. Because – unless you've been living under a rock – you'll know that the cast members of the hit ITV2 show *The Only Way is Essex* are kind, funny, sharp and immaculately groomed from the top of their well-coiffed heads right down to their colour-gelled toenails. We've followed the ups and downs, lives and loves of this glamorous group,

and if there's one thing they've taught us it's to never underestimate an Essex guy or gal.

But let's face it: looking good takes time and effort and needs to be backed up with a firm belief in who you are and what you want – something the *TOWIE* crowd have in spades. We can all stand to learn a few of their tips and tricks, yes, even dry academics trapped behind dusty old desks!

Whether you're an aspiring Essex boy or girl, or have already attained that glorious state, this book is dedicated to you – mwah!

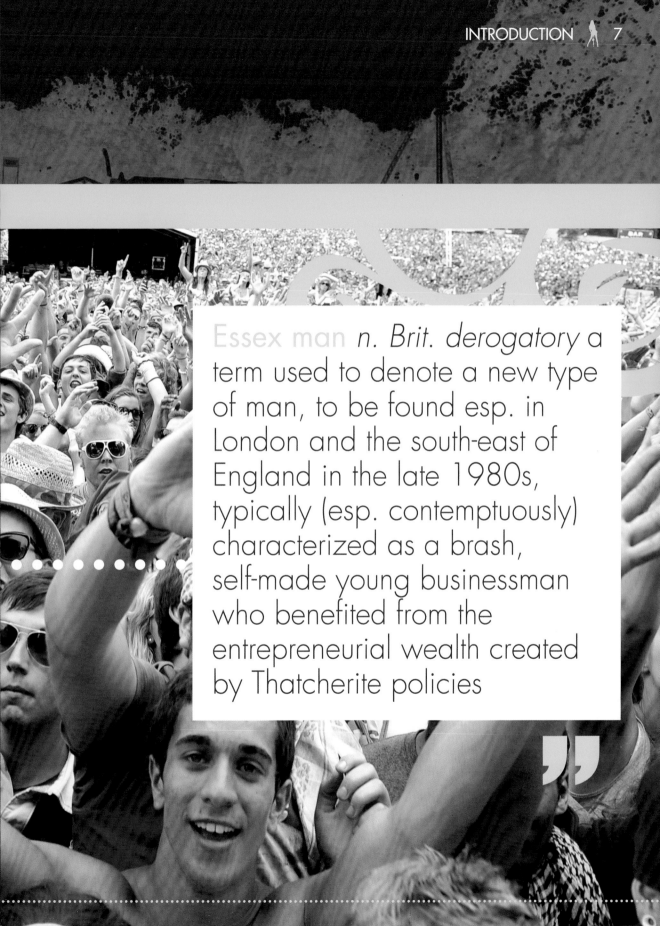

Essex man *n. Brit. derogatory* a term used to denote a new type of man, to be found esp. in London and the south-east of England in the late 1980s, typically (esp. contemptuously) characterized as a brash, self-made young businessman who benefited from the entrepreneurial wealth created by Thatcherite policies

THE CAST

INTRODUCING ... THE CAST

Miss Amy Childs AKA The Sweetheart

Who could say no to her? She has barely an unkind word to say about anyone – all she wants is to see Essex looking its best.

Mark Wright AKA The Jungle Cat

He prowls Essex as if it's his territory and the rest of us are guests in it. And he looks great doing it...

Jessica Wright AKA The Diva

Essex's bona fide pop star is determined to see her dreams come true, and she's determined to do it with good hair and nails.

Harry Derbridge AKA The Babyface

Younger than the rest, little cousin Harry is only just making his name on the Essex social scene. But with a look and moves like his, it won't take him long.

Sam Faiers AKA The ManEater

Already an established model, Sam has more confidence than we've ever seen west of Leyton, and she's not afraid to use it. Beware gentlemen, beware...

Lauren Goodger AKA The Career Girl

She's been nursing a broken heart but has turned it to good by focusing on her career and becoming part of the team behind Essex Fashion Week. We look forward to more feistiness from the woman we'd hate to cross.

Nanny Pat
AKA The Icon

Proving to us that Essex is about graft and home cooking as much as acrylic nails and fast cars, this matriarch has a wise word for whoever might need it – and she won't hold back.

Lucy Mecklenburgh
AKA The
Other Woman

She didn't waste any time in snaffling Mark the minute he was single, but we suspect there's more to her than just being someone's girlfriend.

James 'Arg' Argent
AKA The Crooner

He might not have the lines when he's chatting up the ladies but onstage his silky voice and classic tunes mean the tables are turned. A modern-day Sinatra walks among the Essex folk.

Kirk Norcross
AKA The Host

The cheeky chappy who runs Essex's famous nightspot. Catch him strutting his stuff as Sugar Hut's ultimate host.

Candy Jacobs and
Michael Woods
AKA The Extras

The eyes and ears of Sugar Hut, these two know everything worth knowing.

MARK WRIGHT

Biography

Mr Essex, The Fresh Prince of Brentwood or just 'an ex' – whatever you call Mark, he's the Alpha Male of the Essex universe.

Born in The Royal London Hospital in Whitechapel, Mark comes from a big traditional family headed by the legendary Nanny Pat. His mum is Pat's daughter and his siblings are older sister and LOLA star Jessica, and younger siblings Joshua and Natalia. He also has a fleet of cousins as Nanny Pat has five kids!

Mark spent his early years in Whitechapel before the family moved to the sunny pastures of Chigwell and the Essex dream began. His dad is a football agent and for as long as he can remember Mark has been crazy about football. He paid attention to no classes other than sport at school, and had no interest in any games other than footie. Swings, sandpits and bicycles: BORING! Instead, he devoted his childhood to accidentally smashing his mum Carol's best ornaments with footballs flying in from the garden.

But the practice was worth it as Mark left school at 16 and went to play for Tottenham Hotspur for three years. He played at semi-professional level, and even represented the country at C level. But injury and an uncanny knack of turning a club night into a success led him to retire and focus on what he does best of all: party.

Now a full-time nightclub promoter, he's also a full-time lover of the good life – designer gear, drinks and women. Mr Wright is living the Essex dream, and he's not ashamed to show it off. And we love that.

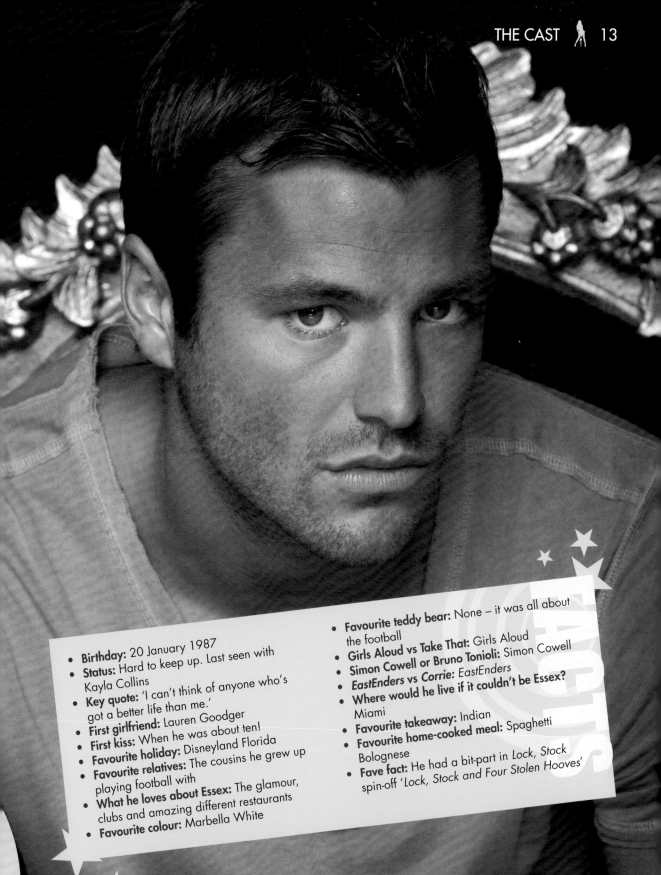

- **Birthday:** 20 January 1987
- **Status:** Hard to keep up. Last seen with Kayla Collins
- **Key quote:** 'I can't think of anyone who's got a better life than me.'
- **First girlfriend:** Lauren Goodger
- **First kiss:** When he was about ten!
- **Favourite holiday:** Disneyland Florida
- **Favourite relatives:** The cousins he grew up playing football with
- **What he loves about Essex:** The glamour, clubs and amazing different restaurants
- **Favourite colour:** Marbella White

- **Favourite teddy bear:** None – it was all about the football
- **Girls Aloud vs Take That:** Girls Aloud
- **Simon Cowell or Bruno Tonioli:** Simon Cowell
- **EastEnders vs Corrie:** EastEnders
- **Where would he live if it couldn't be Essex?** Miami
- **Favourite takeaway:** Indian
- **Favourite home-cooked meal:** Spaghetti Bolognese
- **Fave fact:** He had a bit-part in Lock, Stock spin-off 'Lock, Stock and Four Stolen Hooves'

FACTS

AMY CHILDS

Biography

A heart of gold, a Bambi-like gaze and lips to die for – Miss Amy Childs truly is Essex's sweetheart. Still living at home with her mum, dad and brother Billy, she continues to run her beauty business from 'Amy's Salon' (AKA her garage) while forging her way in the world of modelling.

Amy was born in Barking 20 years ago and now lives in Brentwood. Her dad, a florist who worked seven days a week, was rarely at home during the day and her mum used to cut hair at home. As a baby Amy was somewhat overshadowed by Billy, who was only 19 months older than her and very boisterous. So her favourite occupation was to sit quietly in her high chair while her mum saw to clients, watching the washing machine as if it was a television.

Despite her fascination with kitchen appliances it was the world of beauty that truly captured Amy's imagination. Until she was 11 or 12 she was constantly engrossed in styling her Barbies and Betty Spaghettys with cousin Harry, and after a while they practised their technique by styling each other's hair.

As a schoolgirl she was never in trouble – even becoming head girl. And then she discovered make-up, at which point she was always in trouble for her classroom look: too much tan, too much foundation and too many false eyelashes. Amy kept up with her studies with no problem, and French was her favourite. 'I can't remember any of it, but I know I loved it.' But she would not surrender to anything less than full glamour in the classroom, despite the audience of 'teachers so old that none of them were fit at all'.

So, at 15, Amy started on the path to her dream of glamming up the universe, and began a Saturday job at a local salon. When she left school she attended beauty school in Brentwood for a year and started work full-time as soon as she was qualified. And before long Amy's Salon was born. She might not be able to speak French as well as Sam can speak Spanish, but she wields a spray-tan gun like Clint Eastwood and she's the best friend every girl would like to have.

- **Birthday:** 7 June 1990
- **Family:** Brother Billy
- **Key quote:** 'Beauty is pain.'
- **Favourite holiday:** Disneyland, Florida – Mickey Mouse, Cinderella, all the gang were there
- **Favourite relatives:** Harry
- **What she loves about Essex:** The people, the clothes, and pretty much everything about Brentwood
- **Favourite colour:** What do you think? PINK! Although, she can't wear as much of it as she would like because of her hair
- **Favourite toy:** It's not a toy, but she still carries a comfort blanket around with her. 'It's a little minging blanket but I love it.'
- **Girls Aloud vs Take That:** Take That
- **Simon Cowell vs Bruno Tonioli:** Simon Cowell
- **EastEnders vs Corrie:** EastEnders
- **Where would she live if it couldn't be Essex?:** Dubai
- **The one beauty product she couldn't live without:** YSL false lash effect mascara
- **Favourite takeaway:** Thai
- **Favourite home-cooked meal:** 'I don't do home cooking.'
- **Dream crush:** Her new man Joe

KIRK NORCROSS

Biography

Kirk is the boy from the wrong side of the tracks. Born in Orsett hospital in the 'rough side of Essex', he grew up in Grays – an unglamorous town now made famous by Essex Legend Russell Brand. The maternity ward where he was born was knocked down to make space for a block of flats, but Kirk has done rather better for himself.

Kirk didn't have the same upbringing that a lot of the cast did, and times got harder when his dad, 'a legit Del Boy', left home when he was only a young lad. He suffered from ADHD as a child, and did not do at all well at school. He was a naughty boy in the classroom as he found lessons difficult and one year he had an 87 per cent absentee record. This wasn't because he was up to no good during class time, but because he often preferred to stay at home and help his mum out with shopping and errands.

Once Kirk left school at 16 he tried to take a photography course but he didn't have the grades, so he struggled for a couple of years, trying his hand at various jobs, including welding with his brother, which he hated. Then, four years ago, his dad suggested that he come and work with him on the clubs, and before long Kirk was a bona fide businessman. These days he works 9 to 5 at the Sugar Hut offices, taking care of the business side of things – what looks like a party lifestyle is actually a lot of hard graft.

Happier than he has been for years, he is the ultimate bad boy made good, which makes us love him all the more.

- **Birthday:** 21 April 1988
- **Family:** Older brother Daniel, as well as younger half brother Mason and younger half sister Holly
- **Key quote:** 'The whole world we live in is quite vain.'
- **Favourite holiday:** Pontins with all the family in Yorkshire
- **Favourite relative:** He's always looked up to his dad, and admired how independent his mum is.
- **What he loves about Essex:** Everyone takes proper care about how they look
- **Favourite toy:** He played with Action Men until he was about 13 because he kept getting grounded when he was a teenager
- **Eastenders vs Corrie:** He doesn't like soaps
- **Girls Aloud vs Take That:** Girls Aloud
- **Simon Cowell or Bruno Tonioli:** Simon Cowell
- **Where would he live if it couldn't be Essex?** Florida, because everyone looks as if they know each other there, chatting on their lawns in the sunshine
- **Favourite takeaway:** Indian
- **Favourite home-cooked meal:** His dad has just taught him an amazing paprika chicken recipe, which he can't get enough of
- **Dream crush:** Cheryl Cole

SAM FAIERS

Biography

Sam was a New Year surprise for her parents, and was followed less than two years later by her sister Billie. The family went to live in Marbella, Spain when the girls were young, where Sam and Billie went to school at the aptly named Aloa College. When her builder father had finished work in Spain the family returned to Essex for several years before a second project came up for Mr Faiers in Spain. This time the girls were teenagers though, and they hated being separated from their friends on the exploding Essex social scene, so the family were back to the homeland six months later. Essex: its pull is strong.

As a child Sam was a gymnast training for the Olympic squad. She trained for 4–5 years but it wasn't all leotards and gym mats. She broke her arm three times – once by falling off the kitchen counter at home, once while practising the bars at training and a third time when she had to go to hospital for them to break and re-set it after her previous injuries. Unbelievably, this was not her worst injury. When the family were living in Spain she did a particularly high-spirited forward roll off the sofa and straight into a fancy marble table – slicing her ear nearly clean off in the process. Her mum fainted when she realised it was only hanging on by the lobe and a trip to hospital quickly followed.

Eventually, the injuries proved too much and Sam gave up the Olympic dream but at school her favourite subjects continued to be swimming, netball and PE. She also loved Art and remains a massive fan of Pop Art.

After school Sam got her first job at Lloyds TSB where she worked for two years until Mr Mark Wright introduced her to her new career by suggesting that she enter the *Nuts* Babe 2009 competition. Yeah, we bet he did. Anyway…Sam went on to win and has been modelling ever since.

Things will change in 2011 though as Sam is opening her first boutique, Minnie's on Brentwood High Street this spring. It will sell 'all the dresses that everyone in Essex wants to wear.' We're there…

- **Birthday:** 31 December 1990
- **Family:** Parents Sue & Dave; sister Billie
- **Status:** Single
- **Key quote:** 'I'm an original Marbella Belle'
- **Favourite holiday:** Spain – although it was hardly a holiday
- **Favourite relative:** Sister Billie
- **Favourite colour:** Beige/cream
- **Her favourite thing about Essex:** When you go out, you know you'll know everyone and you'll never, ever be too dressed up.
- **Favourite toy:** A red toy jeep that she used to drive around in while dressed as Pocahontas

- **EastEnders vs Corrie:** Coronation Street
- **Girls Aloud vs Take That:** Girls Aloud because she loves Kimberley Walsh
- **Simon Cowell vs Bruno Tonioli:** Simon Cowell – she and her mum fancy him
- **Where would she live if it couldn't be Essex?** Puerto Banus, Marbella
- **Favourite takeaway:** Chinese
- **Favourite home-cooked meal:** Mum's cooking, especially Shepherd's Pie
- **Dream Crush:** Jason Statham

- **Birthday:** 3 April 1994
- **Status:** Single
- **Key quote:** 'If I ruled the world, everyone would be who they wanted to be'
- **Favourite holiday:** Greece, when he was ten
- **Favourite relative:** Miss Amy Childs
- **What he loves about Essex:** The people and the atmosphere
- **Favourite colour:** Blue
- **Favourite toy:** Barbie

- **EastEnders vs Corrie:** Emmerdale
- **Girls Aloud vs Take That:** Take That
- **Simon Cowell vs Bruno Tonioli:** Bruno
- **Where would he live if it couldn't be Essex?:** Brighton or Soho, 'to be with all the other gays, ha ha!'
- **Favourite takeaway:** Indian
- **Favourite home meal:** Roast chicken
- **Dream crush:** Adam Lambert. Or Will Young. No, Adam...no Will...

HARRY DERBRIDGE

Biography

He might be the youngest in the cast, but he is by no means the least noticeable. With his unique sense of style and his attention-grabbing singing-and-dancing ways, Christmas wishes it were a little bit more camp when it's around Harry.

Born in Romford to parents Karen and John, Harry grew up in Dagenham with his two brothers. As a child he always preferred playing with girls' toys. He used to be shy about buying them though, so when he went shopping with his mum or dad he would say he was getting stuff for his 'cousin Rachel'. 'What would Rachel like?' he'd ask, finger on his chin, before selecting the sparkliest toy on the shelf. There was no cousin Rachel though: it was just part of his dastardly plan to get more and better Barbies than his cousin Amy.

Harry and Amy used to spend hours playing with their Barbies – they had every single version that was released and used to style them to within an inch of their lives. Hair, make-up, outfits: those dolls never looked anything less than beauooooootiful. Harry's mum once tried taking him to football just in case he was missing out, but it quickly became clear that he wasn't bothered: by half-time he had migrated to the side lines and was plaiting all the other mums' hair.

Harry enjoyed school, but mostly because of the dance and drama lessons. He regularly got into trouble for turning up a little (as in, an hour or so) late. But it wasn't because he didn't want to go, but because he had spent the time on perfecting his look. As he explains 'I wasn't skiving, I was making an effort.'

He was 'addicted' to Britney Spears throughout his childhood, and continues to support her every outfit and career choice as long as it's fabulous. But he also has room in his heart for Lady Gaga these days, and considers himself one of her Little Monsters.

He used to work in a hair salon because 'The day I got a Girl's World I was over the moon', but left because there were too many people who weren't prepared to experiment with their look. Now, he's working in a florist, focusing on stardom and dreaming of a world were everyone can do the splits and all dress like Lady Gaga. Try not to let him down, people.

JESSICA WRIGHT

Biography

Like all of the Wright siblings, Jessica was born bang on time. The eldest of Carol's children, she is a responsible big sister – but one with dreams of stardom nevertheless.

She sang her way through childhood, making hundreds of tapes of herself singing on her little pink Talk Girl kit. She even taught herself to use the keyboard she was given and started to write her own songs.

By the time the Spice Girls hit the big time, Jessica knew that she absolutely had to be in a girl band. She took singing lessons throughout school and even attended a stage school from the age of eight. Ballet, theatre, modern dance, tap, acting classes – she took the lot.

However, when Jessica hit 16 and her parents asked her if she wanted to do A levels or go to the Italia Conti stage school, she chose to continue with exams to make sure that she

always had something to fall back on. She got a business degree and a job in marketing before finally realising that her show business ambitions were far from dead and she wanted to give her pop dreams another go.

Now a key member of girl group LOLA, with new management and a single being released soon, Jessica's dream is closer than ever. Will this be her year?

- **Birthday:** 14 September 1985
- **Family:** Siblings Mark, Joshua and Natalia
- **Key quote:** 'Look preened.'
- **Favourite holiday:** Disneyland Florida with all the family
- **Favourite relatives:** Cousin Leah, who she has always looked up to
- **Her favourite thing about Essex?:** You can always go out and get glammed up and you never have to worry about being overdressed
- **Favourite colour:** Pink
- **Favourite toy:** She had a Cabbage Patch doll she adored, but mostly it was singing that she spent her time on

- **Girls Aloud vs Take That:** Girls Aloud
- **Simon Cowell vs Bruno Tonioli:** Simon Cowell
- **EastEnders vs Corrie:** EastEnders
- **Favourite TV Show:** The Only Way is Essex
- **Where would she live if it couldn't be Essex?:** New York
- **Favourite music?** She has always loved Mariah Carey but now she adores Beyoncé and Rihanna for their voices and versatility
- **Beauty product she couldn't live without:** Sun cream for health, but mascara for looks
- **Dream Crush:** Leonardo DiCaprio

SIMON & ADAM RYAN

Biography

Founders of the One Off, One You fashion label, twin brothers Simon and Adam Ryan are big movers on the Essex fashion scene. Not content with simply asking glamorous girls who are down on their luck to try and sell them blue staplers, they have also branched out into wearing 'ferosh' asymmetrical jackets and – perhaps their most noble achievement – setting up the iconic Essex Fashion Week!

Yes, it can't be long before the dynamic duo have replaced Milan with Essex on the international fashion calendar. Our lovely Lauren did a cracking job of setting up their inaugural event at Faces nightclub, even if she maybe-perhaps had her own romantic agenda on the go as well.

We last saw Simon and Adam offering Lauren the opportunity of a lifetime and the chance to move abroad, but she was in two minds about taking it. Will the fashion duo become a trio? Or will The Goodger choose her heart over her head? Either way, we anticipate the boys finding out while wearing jackets that appear to have had their sleeves sewn on back-to-front. Because that's how they roll.

CANDY & MICHAEL

Biography

Candy and Michael are partners in crime at The Sugar Hut, where they both work. Addicted to good hair, good cocktails and juicy gossip, they are the eyes and ears of the club, providing advice and a shoulder to cry on, and an unending stream of banter the rest of the time.

Candy used to be in girl group Red Blooded Women, so she has already had a brush with fame and is happy to take a bit more of a spectator's seat this time. Michael is more interested in playing the field for now.

Candy has had 75 driving lessons and counting. And Michael is the creator of the county's best-named haircut, the Brentwood Swoon.

LAUREN GOODGER

Biography

Lauren was born in the Royal London Hospital in Whitechapel, London. When she was a baby her family lived in Bethnal Green but moved to Essex when she was about seven years old. Lauren's dad, who works in construction, was a big traveller, and as children she and her six brothers and sisters used to go on holidays all over Europe, exploring local sites and restaurants.

Lauren enjoyed school – even though she admits she started paying a bit less attention in class when she met her first boyfriend Mark – and left at 16 in order to train as a hairdresser. She quickly realised that that wasn't the job for her, and headed to London to find a job in the City.

Becoming a corporate PA in one of the big-name banks opened up a whole new world of independence to Lauren, who left home at 20 and soon found herself making new friends, earning decent money and branching out from the world of Essex.

She has combined her skills since, working for Simon and Adam Ryan, and found a way to combine her twin loves of fashion and business in setting up Essex Fashion Week. Now more determined than ever to get over the painful and drawn out break-up of her long-term relationship with Mark, Lauren has her eye on a single goal: life as a successful fashion coordinator.

But does she need to stay with the Ryans to achieve this? Does she have to move abroad? Or can she strike out on her own in more ways than one? After all, if she works for herself she can select all the models for Essex Fashion Week – male and female...

- **Birthday:** 30 September 1987
- **Family:** 4 sisters and 2 brothers
- **Key quote:** 'I'm not a tattoo girl. I just don't like it.'
- **Favourite holiday:** Lanzarote with all the family
- **What she loves about Essex:** The glamour, the boutiques, the bars
- **Favourite Colour:** Pink
- **Favourite toy:** A wooden treasure chest that her dad made, and was filled with Barbies, trolls, and marbles
- **Girls Aloud vs Take That:** Girls Aloud (her sister will be furious she didn't say Take That!)

- **Simon Cowell vs Bruno Tonioli:** Simon Cowell
- **EastEnders vs Corrie:** EastEnders
- **Favourite TV show:** Keeping Up With the Kardashians
- **Where would she live if it couldn't be Essex?:** LA
- **The one beauty product she couldn't live without:** A good moisturiser
- **Favourite takeaway:** Indian
- **Favourite home-cooked meal:** Spaghetti Bolognese – her mum has a special recipe
- **Dream crush:** Brad Pitt, or perhaps Channing Tatum

- **Birthday:** 5 December 1987
- **Status:** Reunited with girlfriend Lydia
- **Family:** Younger sister, Natasha
- **Key quote:** 'I won't spray tan. I've got to be slightly manly.'
- **Favourite holiday:** A trip that took in both Disneyland Paris and Park Asterix
- **What he loves about Essex:** The socialising, as it's a close-knit community
- **Favourite colour:** Black, because it's slimming
- **Favourite toy:** WWF Wrestling action figures
- **Girls Aloud vs Take That:** Girls Aloud
- **Simon Cowell or Bruno Tonioli:** Simon Cowell
- **EastEnders vs Corrie:** EastEnders
- **Where would he live if it couldn't be Essex?** Brighton, where his Nan lives
- **The one beauty product he couldn't live without:** Dove Holiday Skin
- **Favourite takeaway:** Indian
- **Favourite home-cooked meal:** A roast dinner
- **Dream crush:** Michelle Keegan

JAMES 'ARG' ARGENT

Biography

A classic crooner, a devoted boyfriend and loyal mate, James 'Arg' Argent is a man with old-fashioned values, and that's just the way we like him.

James was born in Whipps Cross Hospital, Leytonstone, and was raised in Woodford Green, where he still lives with his family. His dad worked in the City and he too had musical ambitions. Back in the day he was a DJ for parties and he is still known to whip out the vinyl at a fiftieth birthday party if anyone will let him get away with it.

Arg went to Trinity Catholic High School where he was always popular, but never cool. As much of a character then as he is now, he would hang out with the cool gang without letting it rule him. His school days were defined by his time on stage though – a regular at the Kenneth Moore theatre in Ilford, he played the Artful Dodger, David Copperfield, and Edmund from *The Lion, The Witch and the Wardrobe*. He even won a Kenny award – the theatre's equivalent of the Oscars – for Young Performer of the Year.

He left school at 18 after his A levels and wasn't sure what he wanted from a career for a few years. He worked at a stockbroker's, a solicitor's and even at Faces nightclub with Candy for a while.

Then, in the summer of 2007 he met Lydia at a polo event and soon they were a couple. Lydia's mum had a friend who wanted someone singing in their restaurant and at last his dreams of the stage were realised.

When Lydia left school the couple moved to Marbella to work – Arg was singing and Lydia was waitressing. But after a classic 'Ross & Rachael' infidelity (THEY WERE ON A BREAK), the lovers were torn apart. Arg was kicked out and sent back to the UK with his bags packed – depressed, miserable, no job and back with his parents. It was only through *TOWIE* that the couple started talking again and soon old wounds were healed.

These days Arg is getting constant bookings for weddings, christenings, bar mitzvahs, and is even supporting Olly Murs in concert. He's hoping to get a house in Essex with Lydia, and dreams of releasing his own single and going on tour.

LYDIA ROSE BRIGHT

Biography

Lydia was born in Whipps Cross, the same hospital as her beloved James, and lived in Wanstead before the family moved to Woodford when she was five years old. Her dad owns a construction and tiling business and her mum has been fostering children all of Lydia's life.

At school Lydia was a bit of a geek, concentrating on lessons and enjoying learning. She took her A levels at 18 and was planning to take a year off before going on to study English, as she longs to become a writer. For her year off Lydia moved to Marbella with James (she's the only one who calls 'Arg' James), but plans for university were put on hold when they broke up. Now she is concentrating on writing projects and dreams of living the Carrie Bradshaw life. She reckons Arg, sorry – James, is a dead ringer for Mr Big and we reckon she's not far wrong. Here's to the happy couple!

- **Birthday:** 20 January 1991
- **Status:** Back together with boyfriend James 'Arg' Argent
- **Family:** Two real sisters and one real brother, but her mum is a foster carer so there are currently one foster sister and two foster brothers as well. Lydia has had over 200 foster siblings in her life!
- **Key quote:** 'I want to be the next Carrie Bradshaw.'
- **Favourite holiday:** Visiting her Italian mum's family near Ancona
- **What she loves about Essex:** The glamour, and the way that everyone makes a real effort when they go out

- **Favourite colour:** Red
- **Favourite toy:** Barbie and baby dolls
- **Girls Aloud vs Take That:** Girls Aloud
- **Simon Cowell vs Bruno Tonioli:** Bruno Tonioli
- **EastEnders vs Corrie:** Neither
- **Favourite TV show:** Sex & the City
- **Where would she live if it couldn't be Essex?** Opposite Hyde Park
- **The one beauty product she couldn't live without:** Clarins cleanser and toner
- **Favourite takeaway:** Thai
- **Favourite home-cooked meal:** Mum's lasagne
- **Dream crush:** Jude Law or Hugh Grant. The posh English accent every time …

NANNY PAT

Biography

Nanny Pat was born in Bow in 1935, and lived there for 18 years. She grew up knowing just how tough life could be, as the East End of London and the streets around her were bombed during the Second World War. 'In those days there was no social security,' she explains. 'You worked hard or you went hungry. We were all recovering from the war together.' At 18 she met her husband and married him aged 20, at which point they went to live in Canning Town. She had five children in seven years, and Carol, her youngest daughter, is Mark's mum.

For several years she and her husband ran a pub named The Rising Sun in Bromley-by-Bow, before going on to run a greengrocer's and then the local post office. We think it's fair to say that Nanny Pat is a grafter, and there can be little doubt that she and her husband were the eyes and ears of the community.

In 1968 the family moved to Barking, where Nanny Pat started work at the children's school as a cook. South Park Primary School in Ilford must have had the finest school dinners in history, as it was here that Nanny Pat perfected her sausage-plaiting skills, churning out meals for 1,000 pupils at a time. After 27 years at the school, she retired aged 60. Nanny Pat and her husband were married for 52 years, but sadly he died three years ago. Understandably, Nanny Pat was terribly down for some time, but has recently started to enjoy life again. She has even been getting her nails done at the same salon as the girls, and is loving spending so much more time with her grandchildren these days!

- **Birthday:** 1935
- **Key quote:** 'Get on with life, look after yourself and don't do anything silly.'
- **Favourite holiday:** Used to go hop-picking in Kent every September as a child
- **Favourite relatives:** With 14 grandchildren she daren't have favourites!
- **Favourite music:** She loved 'Walking on Sunshine', as sung by Gamu on The X Factor, and she adores Max Bygraves
- **Favourite Colour:** She likes to wear black, but likes reds and a bit of lemon too
- **Favourite toy:** There weren't many in East London during the war, so Nanny Pat used to get last year's doll in a clean frock and love it all the more
- **Simon Cowell vs Bruno Tonioli:** Bruno. She's a big Strictly fan.
- **EastEnders vs Corrie:** Both. And Emmerdale. Nanny Pat loves her soaps.
- **The one beauty product she couldn't live without:** None, she doesn't like too much make-up.
- **Favourite home-cooked meal:** 'I'm not a big eater, but it always tastes delicious if someone else has made it'.

LUCY MECKLENBURGH

Biography

Lucy was born in Romford and has lived in Essex her entire life. She went to school with Sam and has been friends with her ever since. Lucy was a good girl at school – at least compared to her classmate Sam – and when she left she went on to study Business and Accounts at Southend College.

Three years ago Lucy got into the fashion industry, selling clothing wholesale to boutiques. She has had her current job with 'sparkly dressy company' Forever Unique for a year now, and will be working even more closely with Sam in the future.

Watch this space for the future of Essex fashion!

- **Birthday:** 24 August 1991
- **Family:** Two sisters
- **Key quote:** 'Girls, you want to eat the dessert not look like it!'
- **Favourite holiday:** She went on a catamaran around the Caribbean as a teenager
- **What she loves about Essex:** You can get dressed up as much as you want, and no one will think it is too much. In Essex you can get really, really dolled up
- **Favourite colour:** Purple, like my hair
- **Favourite toy:** She used to design and make outfits for Barbies

- **Girls Aloud vs Take That:** Girls Aloud
- **Simon Cowell vs Bruno Tonioli:** Simon Cowell
- **EastEnders vs Corrie:** EastEnders
- **Favourite TV show:** Secret Diary of a Call Girl
- **Where would she live if it couldn't be Essex?:** Canary Wharf or Liverpool
- **The one beauty product she couldn't live without:** Bourjois lipgloss
- **Favourite takeaway:** Thai
- **Favourite home-cooked meal:** Spaghetti Bolognese
- **Dream crush:** Channing Tatum

WHEN ESSEX LIES WITHIN...

They may not be from England's greatest county, but we're prepared to grant them all honorary Essex status....

- **Chelsy Davy** – She's got the hair, she's got the tan, and the lip gloss. You may argue that she's from Zimbabwe, and you can tell us until you're blue in the face that she hangs out with the Royal Family but we all know she's got Essex in her heart.

- **Kanye West** – His love of all things bling is his giveaway symptom.

- **Katy Perry** – She always has great nails, she loves dressing up and she married a boy from Grays. What more do you need to know?

- **Prince Harry** – He loves a party, and a pretty girl. Enough said.

- **Samantha Cameron** – She totally wishes the Houses of Parliament were on Loughton High Road.

- **Blake Lively** – The way she manages to get the perfect balance of leg and cleavage out in any given dress tells us all we need to know.

- **John F. Kennedy** – He had an eye for a beautiful lady, a knack of turning a good party into a money-spinner and a big family he was very close to. He was America's most Essex leader ever.

- **Lady Gaga** – She can go on about being 'Born This Way' as much as she wants but we all know she secretly longs to have been born in Essex.

RELATIONSHIPS

CAST MAP

NANNY PAT!

Family

CAROL WRIGHT

Family

JESSICA WRIGHT

Family

Family

Work

JOSHUA & NATALIA

LOLA

Woof

Ex-Work

BUBBLES

JULIAN FROM UNIVERSAL

LYDIA

Marbella

JAMES 'ARG' ARGENT

Bromance!

MARK WRIGHT

Friends

?

LAUREN GOODGER

Work

CHRIS THE SPEEDATER

Work

SIMON & ADAM RYAN

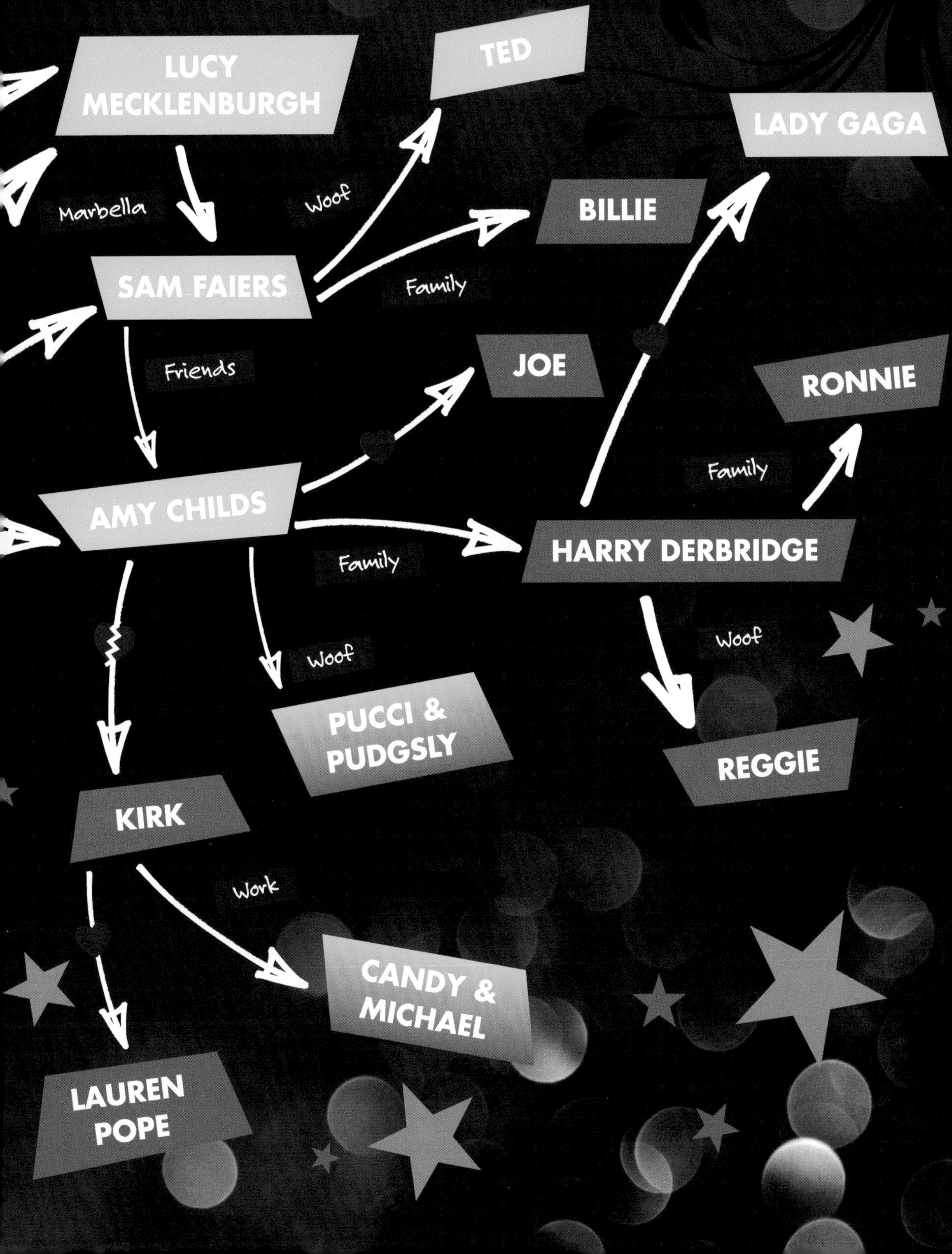

LUCY MECKLENBURGH

TED

LADY GAGA

Marbella

Woof

BILLIE

SAM FAIERS

Family

Friends

JOE

RONNIE

AMY CHILDS

Family

HARRY DERBRIDGE

Family

Woof

Woof

PUCCI & PUDGSLY

REGGIE

KIRK

Work

CANDY & MICHAEL

LAUREN POPE

BROMANCE

Aaaah Mark, while we admire his wolfish way with the ladies, we're not sure we'd like to be on the receiving end of his sharp tongue. As warm as it may be in the sunbeam of his attention, we imagine it's very, very cold in the shade. But there is one side to him that we adore more than any other: the Bromance angle.

With Arg, Mark is an entirely different man – kind, gentle, and attentive. They have been best mates since they were 18 and 19, and while Mark is almost a year older than Arg he is just as prepared to look out for his mates well-being.

From helping to do his hair before a big date to trying to persuade him to wear a wedding dress to help make Halloween extra spooky, Mark is always there for his gentle-hearted bezza.

Arg admits that people think Mark is 'horrible, or arrogant or treats girls like crap, but I know he's got a softer side. He's a good friend and he never lets down me or any of his other friends. He's loyal.'

Mark is keen to keep up his façade, though. All he'd tell us was that he'd 'like to set Arg up with Vicky Pollard.'

Try as hard as you like Mark, we all know there's a softie's heart beating beneath that perfectly smooth chest...

Arg on Mark:

'I've always looked up to him. He's good-looking, he has confidence, he has swagger and he gives me tips on girls, even if it's not always the best advice...'

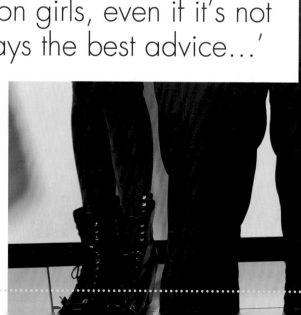

Mark on Arg:
'Don't say that.
If you do, she
will get up
quicker than
you can fart.'

THE WORLD OF ROMANCE: IT'S A BIG-GAME HUNT

There is only one thing you need to know about dating in Essex: it is all about The Chase. The bars and clubs of Chigwell and Loughton are like a safari – predators hidden in every corner, well disguised but ready to pounce at the slightest provocation. As Mark kindly explains: 'We like to do the hunting, otherwise we think the girl's desperate.'

Here are some tips from the cast. Use them at your own risk...

Getting their attention

'Make sure he's in your eyeshot, but don't go up to him. Don't make the first move.' – Jessica

'Eye contact, then ignore. Repeat until you get what you want.' – Sam

'It's all about confidence.' – Amy

The chase

'You've got to have a chase – not forever, it's boring after a while. But there has always got to be a chase.' – Sam

'Don't show anyone that you're interested. That's how I got Mark. He chased me for months.' – Lucy

'I definitely think the Spice Girls influenced our generation, but it's also in us anyway: we don't chase boys, we wait for them to come to us.' – Jessica

'It's all about the chase, you *have* to play a bit hard to get.' – Amy

On the date

'Don't tell too many jokes. There is a difference between reciting jokes and lines, and just being able to make you laugh.' – Amy

'Take care with what you look like. Don't swear. Be yourself. Be chatty. Listen.' – Arg

'You've got to be generous or thoughtful. Try something a bit different – not just your local Pizza Hut.' – Sam

Keeping the flame alive

'Always offer rosé or a glass of champagne, we'll think you're more interesting if you get us a better drink.' – Sam

'Put your phone away. It's rude to keep getting distracted by it.' – Arg

'Don't be clingy or try too hard.' – Mark

Reputation maintenance

'Guys – be a little bit of a player, but don't cross that line.' – Mark

' A best friend would tell their mate if she looks dodgy before a date – truth truth truth is the key.' – Harry

'A big part of it is the chase. But don't play too many games, that's just boring. Difference between playing it cool and playing games.' – Jessica

Also worth remembering

'I am not a good wingman. I am not trustworthy. I would have a go if I wanted to.' – Mark

DEALING WITH A BROKEN HEART – ESSEX STYLE

We've all been there. The romance you thought would never end has come crashing down around your ears and now you're left with a broken heart and a lot of Facebook maintenance to do.

But never fear, because in time-honoured fashion your girls will be there for you – and no one does a girls' night in better than an Essex girl.

What the girls say...

'Your girls will always be there. Keep with your girls, if they're your true friends they'll never turn their back on you.' – Lydia

'Stick with the girls. Go out and get smashed, or stay in and get smashed. But times like this are always girl time.' – Lucy

'Don't change your hair colour. Stay away from the colour. It's not the time for drastic decisions about your new look.' – Amy

Essential kit for an Essex girls' night in

- Wine. A lot of white wine
- A sausage plait and some of Nanny Pat's best Vol-au-vents
- Magazines for pointing out celebrities' flaws
- A DIY vajazzle kit, but NO hair dye
- Music – decent speakers and a girl-power playlist
- Enough nail polish to paint an airplane, in various colours
- A mountain of dresses and shoes to try on, researching new looks for the new you
- Some seriously comfy clothes to put on afterwards. Big, bright hoodies and slippers
- Your beloved dogs and some outfits to dress them up in
- Your pride!

'If it's not meant to be it's not meant to be. Don't look backwards.'
– Amy

THE ESSEX BOY'S GUIDE TO GIRL SPEAK

An Essex girl is a complicated creature. She may seem to know her own mind and tell it like it is, but to the untrained ear it is hard to tell if the men and women are speaking the same language. Understandably, the likes of Mark, Kirk and Arg might need a little help working the girls out. Right? Well, guys, here's some useful tips for getting to know what the girls really want to hear....

'Do you think she is pretty?'

Newsflash: this is a trick question – there is no right answer! Now is the time to distract your gal with something sparkly in the hope that you can change the subject.

'Nothing.'

Nothing is *always* something. And it usually has *everything* to do with you! The only way to proceed at this point is to remember what it is that you did wrong and apologise, quick smart…

'How do I look?'

Her appearance is something that every true Essex girl takes seriously, so it is worth remembering if she has something new; new bag, hair, nails – guys, she wants you to notice and p.s. 'nice' is not good enough here.

'Can you...?'

This is not a question. Yes, you can! Whether it's picking her tiny dog up from the poodle parlor or coming shopping, the answer is always yes. Failure to respond correctly to this question can easily result in 'nothing'.

'Five minutes...'

The Essex girl does not confirm to standard timings, she will be ready when she is ready – whether it takes 5 minutes or 55 minutes, boys, get comfy…

Now that you have the basics down, it is worth taking the time to look over these example situations – practise makes perfect guys...

Example No. 1

WHAT SHE SAYS: 'Yes, I think [insert name here] is pretty.'
WHAT SHE MEANS: 'Tell me I'm more beautiful and that she is an airbrushed, high maintenance, ugly troll.'
WHAT YOU SHOULD DO: Do what she says! Tell her she's beautiful.

Example No. 2

WHAT SHE SAYS: 'What are you doing tonight?'
WHAT SHE MEANS: 'What are you doing with me tonight?' A lot of the time when a woman asks this question her intention is really to make plans for the evening.
WHAT YOU SHOULD DO: Respond with, 'I don't know, did you have something in mind?'

Example No. 3

WHAT SHE SAYS: 'I'm fine.'
WHAT SHE MEANS: 'Things are not fine and I'm mad at you.'
WHAT YOU SHOULD DO: Make a mental note that in a woman's vocabulary the word 'fine' often has the same meaning as 'terrible' and do everything in your power to rectify the situation.

LAUREN & MARK: A RETROSPECTIVE

Every generation has a pair of star-crossed lovers: Romeo and Juliet; Rhett Butler and Scarlett O'Hara; Carrie and Mr Big. Essex is no different. The lip gloss may be stickier and the hair gel may be slicker, but that doesn't dull the heartache. Yes, of course we're talking about Lauren and Mark, the Elizabeth Taylor and Richard Burton of west Essex.

The couple were both born in The Royal London Hospital in Whitechapel and when Lauren's family moved to Essex in the early 1990s they lived only a road away from the Wrights. Mark says he can remember Lauren as his ten-year-old neighbour, but Lauren's first memory of him is when they were at school together as teenagers. At fifteen they became a couple and soon they were spending all their time together – bunking off school to head to Loughton High Road, texting each other during classes and becoming the unofficial king and queen of their year at school.

Prom night had no appeal to them though – the couple did not attend when they left school, preferring to head to Spain for their first holiday together. This was where Lauren met the rest of Mark's extended family and was the first of many happy holidays for them.

But after nine years the couple decided to separate. Mark wanted his freedom after such a long relationship and Lauren felt that she deserved to be treated better than she had been. Everyone's first love is hard to get over, but to go through a break up on national television makes it even harder. There's a part of them that will always be each other's but will they every truly be reunited? Only time will tell...

He says... 'I don't know what Lauren's up to these days'.

She says... 'We're not over. We're just not over.'

THE WISDOM OF NANNY PAT

It's all very well taking a peek at the glamorous lives of the Essex A-list, but we all know the show wouldn't be the same without Nanny Pat. And it's not just her sausage plait that makes her iconic – it's her words of wisdom. Here are some of her greatest comments on modern living. Nanny Pat, we salute you.

'Get on with life, look after yourself and don't do anything silly'.

On her late husband: 'Fifty-two years we were married, now that's a marriage. He would have loved the show ... and taken it over'

'I hate all the swearing that goes on today. I just wish people could be a bit more ladylike.'

On running a pub in the east end after the Second World War: 'Them days was hard. We was all recovering from the war together.'

'I never drink. Well, I have the odd shandy...'

On matters of the heart: 'If you don't like a girl you tell her, and if you like her tell her. Be more straightforward.'

'I like nice nails and I like nice hair extensions on the girls.'

On her grandchildren's hangovers: 'I bring them bacon sandwiches now, that always helps.'

I just keep myself fit by getting life done – running around after the grandchildren is enough.'

GROOMING

BIGGER, BOLDER, BETTER!

We all know the best thing about Essex by now: it's that if you're getting dressed for a big night out, there is no 'too much'. You never, ever have to worry about overdoing it. Heels, hair colour, corsets – let your imagination run wild! If you're going to go out looking Essex, you're going to have to embrace the art of extending, and holding it tight.

Lashes

Whatever your means, your lashes must be extended. This is crucial. An unadorned lash has not been seen on Loughton High Road since the summer of 1976.

- Lauren is the only one of the girls who doesn't wear false eyelashes, preferring to use Dior Shadow mascara.
- Jessica is a slave to the Girls Aloud range of eyelashes, but it's the Nadine or Sarah Harding ones that are Jessica's fave.
- Amy recommends strip lashes or individual lashes, but believes that permanent lash extensions can damage your natural lashes.

Hair

You've heard all the hair extension horror stories and now you're petrified that you'll end up bald, ugly and a lot poorer? Well, if you don't do your homework then of course this could happen. But there's a way to have beautiful hair using hair extensions without damaging your own hair, and in fact allowing your natural hair to grow longer and healthier in the process.

Our *TOWIE* girls would always recommend getting a professional to do your hair extensions or using clip on as a quick fix for a night out on the town. Whether you go straight, wavy or curly; always think vibrant, voluminous and voluptuous.

'Essex girls don't wear make-up because they're ugly but because it's polite – it's just making an effort. Why wouldn't you?' – Harry

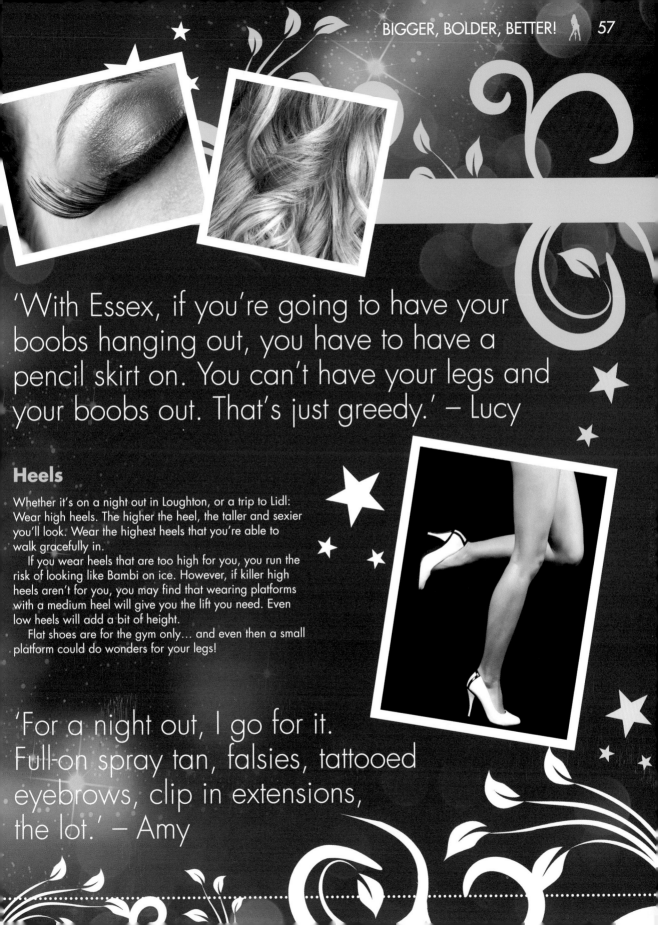

'With Essex, if you're going to have your boobs hanging out, you have to have a pencil skirt on. You can't have your legs and your boobs out. That's just greedy.' – Lucy

Heels

Whether it's on a night out in Loughton, or a trip to Lidl: Wear high heels. The higher the heel, the taller and sexier you'll look. Wear the highest heels that you're able to walk gracefully in.

If you wear heels that are too high for you, you run the risk of looking like Bambi on ice. However, if killer high heels aren't for you, you may find that wearing platforms with a medium heel will give you the lift you need. Even low heels will add a bit of height.

Flat shoes are for the gym only… and even then a small platform could do wonders for your legs!

'For a night out, I go for it. Full-on spray tan, falsies, tattooed eyebrows, clip in extensions, the lot.' – Amy

NAILING IT

Nails: more than make-up, more than accessorising, for the women of Essex nails are a way of life. As relaxing as going for a bed and yet requiring as much attention as a chug, they should take up as much time as is needed, but every second is worth it. Let's face it: in Essex a regular manicure isn't a treat but a necessity. Get to know all there is to know about the selection of manicures available to you.

Four hot looks for your nails

Painted

This is Lauren's preferred method, and she has an impressive wardrobe of colours. Her manicures are in Jessica or Chanel beige or mushroom tones for most of the year, but in summer she likes to go with an orange or a coral. This season she has been mostly working a mushroom nail with a single Swarovski crystal on the tip.

Acrylics

Amy wears acrylic nails, usually with a white tip to create the French Manicure effect. She finds that they last longer than anything else on her hands as she works with so many chemicals in her salon. Anything else just gets ruined too quickly.

Jessica also wears acrylic nails, although more often painted than not.

Lauren, however, cannot stand acrylic nails – especially the white-tipped ones.

Colour gels

These are thick gels that are applied to the nails and dry rock solid – they last up to three weeks. Sam is a huge fan of colour gels. Her fingers and toes are always matching and she has the colour changed once every three weeks.

Minx Nails

Currently Lucy's favoured look, Minx nails are when patterned or metallic images are stuck onto the nail beds with strong, heated glue. It's the technique Katy Perry used to get a manicure with ten tiny images of Essex Icon Russell Brand's face. We look forward to a generation of 'Kirk' Minx manicures in the near future…

What the cast say:

'Matching nails are unbelievably important.' – Amy

'I like long hands. I don't like too much colour but I do like false nails on a girl.' – Mark

'Nails are the key – they're always on show. Nothing worse than grubby nails.' – Jessica

'Always, always make sure that toe and fingernails are matching. It's a minor detail but it's worth it.' – Sam

Nail Fact

Nanny Pat didn't use to have time for manicures but since her husband died she has taken to going to the same salon as the girls and getting brightly coloured acrylic nails done, which really cheer her up.

THE LAWS OF LIP GLOSS

Application is meditation

Hours can be spent applying and reapplying. It is a way of readying oneself for a busy day ahead, an important date or, of course, just a quick workout down the gym.

Too much is never enough

If you can't press your lips together and feel what seems to be two gummy bears kissing, you're not wearing enough.

Breeze is your enemy

Beware the wind if you value your hair extensions. Nothing can stop a day in its tracks faster than a strong breeze and a chunk of hair getting stuck to your lips. If in doubt, purse your lips while walking from bar to car.

It's not about how it makes you look, it's about how it makes you feel

Let's face it: Lip gloss tastes good and life is better when you're wearing it.

Feel the tube

There's nothing like the sense of power gained from wearing a tight outfit and knowing that there is still space for your gloss in one of the pockets. It's like being armed. Be ready to draw your weapon at a moment's opportunity.

Essex is not a red-lipped county

You can wear whatever shade you want, as long as it's pink. Seriously – rose pink, shell pink, candy pink, baby pink. But. Just. Not. Red.

Amy's Guide to an Instant Pout:

'Look natural, feel good about yourself, be confident and relax your lips. Then perhaps open your mouth a little bit'

Don't forget your lines

Lipliner, ladies, it's a must. Just be careful not to go too much darker than your gloss shade, or you might look a bit too 'adult'.

Lick the glass

Don't lose your gloss to your drink – lick the rim of the glass first and the gloss won't stick. This should look sexy, not as if you're absent-mindedly about to eat the glass itself.

A beach holiday is just a chance for lip exfoliation

Don't get depressed when your favourite Juicy Tube comes home covered in sand. Seize the opportunity! You haven't ruined a lip gloss, you've gained an exfoliating product.

Boy oh boy, what is he thinking?

Some like the look, some like the taste. But you'll never know until you try. We're sorry we can't help you out more here, but you're just going to have to kiss the guy to find out what he thinks about lip gloss. Good luck!

THE WORLD OF VAJAZZLING

Vajazzling – to many it is simply the act of making your vajayjay bedazzling, but in Essex it is a way of life. In a world where everything should be made as sparkly as it possibly can be, one's lady garden is no exception.

But ladies – don't fall into the trap of thinking that vajazzling is a necessity when it comes to attracting the attention of gentlemen. It is simply self-adornment done for fun and self-expression.

Types of vajazzle

The professional vajazzle

There are two types of vajazzle – the professional and the DIY vajazzle. The type that we see Amy administering in the show is of course the professional vajazzle. These last much longer, but they involve hot, professional-use-only glue. Amy recommends that you leave it to the professionals – find someone with a 'clean salon and a steady hand' – and make sure that they are wearing gloves. This way, getting your vajazzle will be a relaxing experience and the design itself will last longer. Remember Miss Childs' words of wisdom: 'It just isn't as simple as putting on false eyelashes.'

A further warning if you're going for a professional vajazzle: make sure that you have a patch test a couple of days before, to check that you are not allergic to the glue. Finding out about an allergy after you've been vajazzled for a special occasion could, as Amy points out, 'lead to a seriously bad weekend away.'

The Do-it-Yourself

If you are conducting a DIY vajazzle there are lots of designs to choose from and lots of areas to adorn.
Here is our step-by-step guide to DIY vajazzling.

1. Make sure your working area is smooth. That's right, clean skin, a wax or a nice clean shave please.
2. Wipe the area with the little surgical wipe supplied (not champagne) or witch hazel, and dry well.
3. Carefully peel back the white backing away from the crystal design, or trace the outline onto the skin, if you are
   unsure of going 'freestyle' with your design.
4. Firmly press the crystals on your skin with your hand for 10 – 15 seconds. The heat of your hand will make them stick
   to your skin.
5. Slowly peel off the transparent sheet at a flat angle and firmly press the crystals on your skin again.

Note: You can further enhance your vajazzle by trimming your pubic hair into specific shapes and even dyeing it. But
Amy reckons 'that's just getting a bit too involved for me'. And we agree.

For fans of the show who want a little extra sparkle, look out for a range of *The Only Way is Essex* inspired vajazzle
body art crystal designs soon to be available from **www.vajazzle.me.uk** (the UK and Europe's official supplier).
Good luck and happy vajazzling!

VAJAZZLE DESIGNS: A VAJAZZLE FOR ALL OCCASIONS

How to vajazzle to the max, whatever the weather.

New Year's Eve:	Fireworks, in a multicoloured design. Truly, it will be like Big Ben on the Thames.
Valentine's Day:	Hearts. Or perhaps a bunch of roses if you have the number of a bold vajazzle technician.
A Beach Holiday:	Amy advises that you can show your vajazzle to more than just your beloved when on holiday, with a beach ball or dolphin design rising from your bikini bottoms.
Christmas:	'Holly leaves, or perhaps a couple of baubles' are Sam's suggestion for the festive season.
Halloween:	A pumpkin. But please, not a witches hat. Have some dignity, ladies!
Birthdays:	A wrapped present makes a cute hint…
The Royal Wedding:	It would be appropriate to celebrate the happy couple's big day with a vajazzle of their new crest of arms, but if you can't make that we're sure a Union Jack would do.
Anniversary:	As Sam explains: 'A pair of lips is fine for a cheeky weekend away, but if it's your anniversary you could get his initials as that's more respectful'.

Great vajazzles of our time

It's a well-kept Essex secret, but here are some famous heroines from history and the vajazzles that they rocked beneath their robes…*

Queen Elizabeth I	The Virgin Queen was a fan of discreet lacy designs, and the odd ruffle pattern.
Amelia Earhart	Amelia indulged in a small airplane design following her success in being the first woman to fly across the Atlantic.
Florence Nightingale	A lamp, as a nod to the nickname 'The Lady with the Lamp' that the famous nurse was given by *The Times*.
Margaret Thatcher	The Iron Lady used to be vajazzled with the figures of the national debt as a way of keeping her inspired.
Cleopatra	Cleo went with a pyramid. It wasn't great, to be honest, but she did a lot of good work for ancient eye make-up so we can't be too harsh.

* These vajazzles are totally fictitious, but wouldn't they be amazing!

VAJAZZLE GOLDEN RULES – DOS AND DON'TS

Whilst the popular placement of vajazzle crystals in Essex is somewhere a little more intimate, it is important to remember that vajazzles can be used all over your body.

These gorgeous gems are not restricted to your nether regions; why not add some sparkle to your face, neckline and shoulders or at the base of your back to compliment that little black dress? Or add a little sex appeal to your bikini beach look, and glam up your ankles. The possibilities are endless!

However, there are some golden rules to follow wherever you decide to embellish...

 DO

DO wear your vajazzles all over your body. These gorgeous gems are not restricted to your nether regions – why not add some sparkle to your face, neckline and shoulders or at the base of your back to compliment that little black dress? Or add a little sex appeal to your bikini beach look and glam up your ankles.

DO make sure that the vajazzle on your vajayjay is only visible to those you want to see it. No one wants an errant vajazzle.

DO only let someone with appropriate qualifications vajazzle you. It's a delicate business – as Amy says 'It can get dangerous'.

DO approach others with caution when vajazzled. Scratching your sweetheart is not a good look.

DO choose the right vajazzle design for the occasion, there's plenty to choose from. And if you're going to spell out your beloved's name, make sure you have spelled it correctly. A misspelled vajazzle is no way to find out your girlfriend isn't that into you.

DO remember that vajazzling should be fun, fashionable and not an obligation.

✗ DON'T

DON'T stay in a vajazzle salon if you think it looks dirty. Say no-no to minging tweezers near your noo-noo.

DON'T vajazzle near to small children. The jewels are too tempting for them. It is a potential choking hazard and a waste of Swarovski.

DON'T bathe when vajazzled as crystals could fall off. A quick shower is best.

DON'T vajazzle drunk. The rules of drunk texting apply here. Whatever it is, it won't be as funny in the morning.

DON'T have a matching his & hers vajazzles. There are better ways to show your love.

HAIR

There is only one hair rule to follow in Essex: BIG. It doesn't matter what your hair looks like, as long as it has been teased as far as it can possibly go. Everyone works hard in Essex and their hair is no exception.

For her

The key here is extensions. Layer upon layer of them. They build length, volume, and attitude.

Jessica prefers big voluminous hair over length. Cheryl Cole is her hair icon, although she does like a good up-do too.

Amy is a fan of clip-on extensions, because of their flexibility. Her three step rule is: 'Back comb the crown, slip them in, and brush over the join. No one wants to look like Britney on a bad hair day.'

How you extend is not important, but doing so is. All Essex boys like girls with long hair, and all Essex girls like it even longer than that. Big hair: no excuses.

For him

Think Mark at the 60s night. Think Don Draper. THAT is the look you're aiming for. Yes, people, think wet-look. As Mark told Arg as he tenderly teased his perfect wet-look hair: 'Now you look like a bird magnet.' What greater compliment could a man give his fellow Essex boy? But remember: it can't be crispy. As Amy warns 'Loughton boy wet-look is good – but you don't want to worry that you might get your hand caught in it.'

The Alternative: the Brentwood Swoon

Michael Woods never seems that busy behind the bar at Sugar Hut but he does have fabulous hair. For those of you who don't fancy the standard wet-look, a Brentwood Swoon is the next best thing.

You will need: mousse, hairspray and a decent brush.

1. Apply a generous helping of mousse to the hair, root to tip.
2. Dry using the brush to lift the hair on end as you hold the hairdryer to the roots. Tip your head upside down for extra volume if necessary.
3. Once the hair is dry, use the brush to sweep the hair up and back from the forehead, creating the famous swoon.
4. NOW SPRAY. Spray! Spray as if your life depends on it! And then leave it. Don't brush the hairspray out or volume may be lost.

TANNING

Essex – a county not known for its year-round sunshine. And yet ... well known for its year-round tans. No one wants to look unhealthy. Whether you're getting sprayed with lotion or going for a bed, the message is the same: you've got to make the effort. Take your pick from our selection of shades. You know you want to.

HONEY-DEW MELON
A light, more golden orange for the starter tanner.

AMBER
Increasing the golden glow for those getting more confident on the tan-slopes.

WHISKEY
You're ready for Loughton High Road now. Just make sure you're wearing a short-enough skirt or a low-enough shirt to show off your new colour.

MARMALADE
My colour? Oh, I just caught the sun at the weekend…

LUCOZADE SPORT
Moving from just 'well bronzed' to 'well Essex' this stage marks true commitment from a high-level tanner.

SATSUMA
The satsuma can only really be reached by multiple, panicked spritzes of fake tan applied straight from the can to the face halfway through a particularly good night out. You're in deep now.

PUMPKIN
The point at which you start to glow in the dark, as if left on a doorstop at Halloween. Be proud.

EASYJET
If your face is the same colour as one of Stelios' signs you have reached the high point of all orangeness. Buy yourself a Tango cocktail and pat yourself on the back.

THE MAHOGANY
Marking the transition point from orange to truly deeply brown. If you don't powder your forehead you can achieve the complete coffee-table gleam.

THE GUINNESS
Bronzed perfection, and with some nice highlights you too can pull off a complete 'Guinness'.

"What the cast say:

'I hate fake tan. I only like sun beds, because that's a normal tan - a real tan.' – Mark

'I love having a spray tan. San Tropez is the best. I don't use sun beds.' – Jessica

'Sometimes I use a sun bed, and sometimes Amy does me a spray tan, or I just keep a bottle of Fake Bake at home for emergencies.' – Harry

'I like a full on spray tan. I like it dark.' – Amy

'I used to be addicted to sun beds when I was a teenager. At one point I was a deep purple.' – Lucy

'In Essex everyone does have a bit of a colour – we just look better with a bit of colour.' – Lauren

'Essex girls have a year-round tan, there is no way of telling if it's summer or winter when you look at us.'– Lucy "

Tanned heroes

Eva Mendes, Jessica Alba, Nicole Sherzinger, Cheryl Cole

TAN GUIDE

TATTOOING

Whether you're getting your loved one's name written somewhere very intimate, or just getting a massive image of her across your leg, Essex tattoos make as much of an impact as every other part of your look.

There is a lot of tanned, toned flesh in the Golden County, so not to decorate it would be shameful, but go easy, it's not for everyone...

What do the cast think...?

Sam has a tattoo in a secret place on her body that nobody knows about and says: 'Don't get too complicated, there's no need for it to get complicated.'

'Getting them done on your back is fine, but it's a no to tattoo sleeves. Well, they do just look a bit like sleeves, don't they?'
Amy

'I'm not a tattoo girl. I just don't like it.'
Lauren

'Too much is, well,
it's too much isn't it?
It can all get a bit
Pete Doherty slash
someone else,
can't it?'
Amy

MAP OF THE WORLD

Amy's Salon, Brentwood

Some call it Amy's Salon. Other's call it 'Amy's garage'. In truth, it is both – she converted the family garage to make it her own and now that it is decorated with a sufficient level of pink it's one of the hottest beauty destinations in the county. It's hard to leave unvajazzled.

Brentwood High Street, Brentwood

If it can't be found on Brentwood High Street, it's not worth having.

Buddha Beach Bar, Puerto Banus, Marbella

Think of this as Faces in the sun. With fewer clothes.

Crystal Lounge, Loughton

One of Jessica's favourite venues, this is another lynchpin of the Essex social scene. Of *course* it is, it's sparkly…

David Lloyd, Chigwell

Where Mark works out, so ladies – make sure you've got your best bikini on if you're heading to the outdoor swimming pool this summer.

Deuces Bar & Lounge, Chigwell

What's a Saturday night without Deuces? It isn't Saturday night…

The King William, High Road Chigwell

A classic date venue – although, perhaps a risky one if your name is Mark Wright and you don't fancy bumping into any exes.

Faces nightclub, Ilford

A legend more than a location, Faces has played host to some of the greatest and most Essex nights in the county's history. To go there is truly to live.

Marbella

The sunny sister of Essex, this Spanish town is basically Essex-on-Sea, and therefore it deserves a place on the map of Essex.

Mars & Venus salon, Brentwood

A favourite of Amy and Harry's, this is one of Essex's beauty hotspots, and the inspiration for Amy's Salon.

Minnie's Boutique, on Roper's Yard

A newcomer on the Essex map, this is Sam Faiers' first foray into the world of fashion. As she puts it, Minnie's will sell 'all the dresses that everyone in Essex wants to wear', so grab your wallet…

Nu Bar

A favourite with all the girls – just make sure you order your date champagne or rosé. No messing, lads.

Ocean Club, Puerto Banus, Marbella

Exclusive beach club, ideal for surveying who has really caught the sun since arriving in Spain…

Road to London

For access to Lipsy headquarters, film premieres, and China Whites.

Sugar Hut

Kirk's empire, and rival night out to Deuces. Sugar Hut slightly has the edge by having everyone's favourite Slug & Lettuce right in front of it.

Virgin Active Gym, Chigwell.

This is Amy's fitness choice, as she reckons it's cleaner, and she's 'heard a lot of stories about other gyms' changing rooms'… She also used to work here.

GOING OUT

ESSEX HAPPY HOUR

There is nothing our Essex boys and girls like better than unwinding after a hard day's work, and whether it's getting together with your besties for a full-on gossip-fest, or partying the night away at Faces, nothing says relaxation quite like the first sip of a fabulous cocktail. Here are our recommendations for recreating the ambiance of Nu Bar in your living room.

Marbella Sunrise

Inspired by all the Marbella belles and beaus, you can just imagine the reds and oranges of a typical Marbella sunset over the beach... bottoms up!

Ingredients
- 1 part tequila
- 4 parts orange juice
- 1 part grenadine

Method
Fill a tall glass with ice. Pour in the tequila and add the orange juice. Mix. Carefully pour in the grenadine, allowing it to slip to the bottom. It will gradually work its way up a little giving the drink a reddish glow.

The Classic Cosmo

Perfect for a girl's night in, this is the ultimate drink for you and your BFFs. Consume whilst watching back-to-back *Sex and the City* episodes!

Ingredients
- 1½ measures vodka
- 1 measure Cointreau
- 1 measure cranberry juice
- Juice of ½ limes
- Slice of lime to decorate

Method
Add the vodka, Cointreau, cranberry and lime juice into a cocktail shaker, add ice and shake. Strain into a martini glass and add a slice of lime to garnish. Carrie Bradshaw, eat your heart out!

Jelly Shots

Just like the *TOWIE* cast, this little treat is perfectly formed, a real crowd pleaser and a good way to liven up any night.

Ingredients

- 20g gelatine
- 80ml hot water
- 30ml cold water
- 50ml your favourite alcohol

Method

Add hot water to the gelatine and stir until dissolved. Mix in the cold water then add your tipple of choice. You may also want to add some bright food colouring. Divide between shot glasses and refrigerate before serving.

Tip

Cut oranges in half and scoop out the flesh. Fill with the jelly mixture and leave to set. Cut into quarters to serve.

Bourbon Sour

Inspired by our very own James 'Arg' Argent, this is definitely one for the old school crooners.

Ingredients

- 2 measures bourbon
- Juice of half a lemon
- ½ tsp sugar
- Orange slice and a cherry to garnish

Method

Mix all ingredients in a cocktail shaker with ice. Strain into a tall glass and garnish with the fruits.

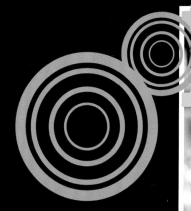

The 'Wright' Russian

After a long night playing host to the Essex glitterati nothing could be more relaxing than this indulgent late night drink.

Ingredients
- 1½ measures vodka
- 1 measure coffee liqueur
- 1 measure cream

Method
Add the vodka, coffee liqueur, cream and ice into a cocktail shaker and shake once or twice, then strain over an ice filled rocks glass and decorate with a cherry.

The Morning After Bloody Mary

What you need the morning after the night before…

Ingredients
- 1 measure vodka
- 3 measures tomato juice
- 2 dashes Worcestershire sauce
- 2 dashes of Tabasco sauce
- 1 dash of fresh lemon juice

Method
Add all the ingredients plus salt and pepper into a cocktail shaker, add ice and shake well. Strain into a glass filled with ice and serve with a stick of celery. Voilà!

DIY PARTY PLANNING

When hosting a soirée Essex style, it isn't enough to simply serve up some pineapple on sticks and a few cold cocktail sausages. To get the Essex stamp of approval you'll need to go a little further and make the effort. With a splash of creativity and a dash of know how, you'll be able to pull off a faultless night to remember!

It's all in the planning...How to be the perfect party host or hostess

When getting ready to host the party of the season, a little planning beforehand goes a long way. Follow these simple steps to make your event go with a bang:

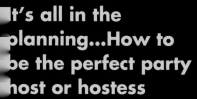

- Pick a date well in advance. A Friday or Saturday night will guarantee a bigger turnout.
- Decide who you're going to invite. A mix of old and new friends works well – but pick carefully: you don't want your ex turning up with his new girlfriend on his arm. Drama at your party is no good if you're at the centre of it.
- Put the word out at least three weeks in advance. Receiving a proper invite through the post,

especially if it's unexpected, is all the more exciting – but a text or Facebook invite will do the job. State times, dress code and what to expect in the way of food and drinks. If you're having a themed party, this is the time to let people know.
- Make sure you leave enough time to prepare your venue, but most importantly prepare yourself. Remember that you are the host and should be centre of attention – hair, nails, clothes and make-up should be thought of well in advance and time for pampering on the day should be factored in.

Themes

Everyone in Essex loves to dress up, so having a theme for your party is the perfect way to get your guests in the mood and excited about your event. Here are our suggestions:

Beach Party
Well, it's one sure-fire way to see potential dates in their swimwear…

Superheroes
Who will be the Clark Kent to your Lois Lane?

James Bond
Nothing sexier than a group of slick Essex boys in their finest dinner suits, and a great excuse for the ladies to splash out on a new fab frock.

Saints and Sinners
Time to get cheeky, but are you a delicious devil or an innocent angel?

Traffic Light Party
Give people stickers on their way in: red means taken, amber means maybe and green means GO, GO, GO!

Old School Hollywood
Why not take a leaf out of Arg's book and remember the good old days of Frank Sinatra and Dean Martin, or better yet book him in to serenade your guests.

Bollywood
Why not recreate this brilliant moment from series one and throw your own *TOWIE* inspired Bollywood night.

THE ESSENTIAL ESSEX TOP TENS!

A Girls' Night In

Whether it's a DIY-vajazzle night or an evening in with a heartbroken mate, you're going to need the perfect selection of music and films if you're going to do it the Essex way.

MUSIC TO DANCE TO
1. 'Just Dance' – Lady Gaga
2. 'Hold It Against Me' – Britney Spears
3. 'Simply the Best' – Tina Tuner
4. 'Firework' – Katy Perry
5. 'Champion' – Chipmunk ft. Chris Brown
6. 'Girls Just Want To Have Fun' – Cindy Lauper
7. 'Only Girl' – Rihanna
8. 'Moment 4 Life' – Nicki Minaj
9. 'Hung Up' – Madonna
10. 'Wannabe' – Spice Girls

MUSIC TO GET OVER HIM
1. 'I Will Survive' – Gloria Gaynor
2. 'Since You Been Gone' – Kelly Clarkson
3. 'Fight For This Love' – Cheryl Cole
4. 'Not Fair' – Lily Allen
5. 'Fighter' – Christine Aguilera
6. 'Single Ladies' – Beyoncé
7. 'Hot 'n' Cold' – Katy Perry
8. 'Independent Women' – Destiny's Child
9. 'I Hate You So Much Right Now' – Kelis
10. 'I Don't Need a Man' – Pussycat Dolls

ESSENTIAL GIRLIE FILMS
1. The Notebook
2. Grease (1 & 2)
3. Legally Blonde (1 & 2)
4. Dirty Dancing
5. Pretty Woman
6. Save The Last Dance
7. Sex and City: The Movie
8. Clueless
9. Mean Girls
10. Titanic

A Night Out

Looking to create your own Deuces? We're sorry we can't help you with Sam on door or Arg on hand for a moment's crooning, but here's a handpicked playlist of guaranteed floor fillers… and a handful that must be avoided at all costs.

CLUB PLAYLIST
1. 'Deuces' - Chris Brown
2. 'Show Me Love' - Robin S
3. 'What's My Name' – Rihanna
4. 'Up In The Club' - Marques Houston ft. Joe Budden
5. 'Club Can't Handle Me' – Flo Rida ft. David Guetta
6. 'Bad Romance' – Lady Gaga
7. 'Tick Tock' – Ke$ha
8. 'Do It Like a Dude' – Jessie J
9. 'Pass Out' – Tinie Tempah
10. 'Yeah!' – Usher

ATTENTION! THESE ARE TO BE AVOIDED AT ALL COSTS

1   S Club 7
2   Phil Collins
3   Lemar
4   STEPS
5   Slipknot

Driving Music

It goes without saying that our *TOWIE* crew love to match their shiny cars with the right soundtrack. Here are our suggestion of artists who sounds great on the car stereo, but make sure the windows are down and the music is loud when you're driving around...

Usher
Rihanna
Tinie Tempah
Plan B
Chipmunk
N'Dubz
Eminem
Dr Dre
Snoop Dogg
Lady Gaga

TOP 10 DATE MOVIES

1   Anything starring Channing Tatum – our gorgeous *TOWIE* girls can't get enough of this piece of eye candy
2   *50 First Dates*
3   *The Notebook*
4   *Notting Hill*
5   *Jerry McGuire*
6   *Love, Actually*
7   *He's Just Not that Into You*
8   *The Holiday (best around Christmas)*
9   *P.S. I Love You*
10   *Gone With The Wind*

SHOPPING THE ESSEX WAY

There's shopping. And then there's shopping the Essex way. Do it in style, ladies, you know you want to.

- Find boutiques that you like. Check out your local high street for independent retailers who will remember you and your style. Turning up at Nu Bar in the same Karen Millen number as two other girls is not a good look.

- Never try on party dresses without the right accessories. Take a pair of heels, a strapless bra and something with which to tie up your hair so you can get an idea of the whole party look. Trying on a tulip skirt when you can see sock marks on your ankles is off-putting.

- Don't be bullied into buying anything. Remember, a lot of sales assistants work on commission, and some of them will tell you almost anything to get a sale. Either take a good mate who knows your style or make sure the shop knows what you're looking for before they start bringing you ugly dresses.

- Avoid the high street on a Saturday unless you enjoy the attention. You're bound to bump into someone you know, so make sure that you don't mind them seeing you try on a skirt that gives you muffin top or a dress that makes you look like a surf board.

- And remember: no trip to the shops has been completed until you've visited the nail bar. Whether it's minx, acrylics or colour gels, a shopping trip isn't a shopping trip without a manicure.

GET THE ESSEX BOY LOOK

Amateurs may think that the perfect Essex boy look is a matter of a big watch, a pair of shiny shoes and a bucket of hair product. The fools. The Essex-man look is about sophistication. It's about pride, it's about masculinity, and it's about *really* big watches. Here are some tips from the cast on how to take it to the next level.

What the cast say...

'The main thing is to have nice teeth. Lovely, white, neat teeth.' – Sam

'Go to the gym at least twice a week to make sure that you feel good about yourself.' – Amy

'Make sure you have the right amount of hair: somewhere between getting rid of your unibrow and shaving your chest entirely.' – Lucy

'Even if you're working a retro look, be neat with it. No one likes a scruff.' – Lauren

'Don't be overly fashionable or too complicated. Making more effort than your date is not a good look. I like to be the one in the fancy stuff.' – Sam

'Nails need to be short but not necessarily manicured. Long nails, especially toenails, are a terrible look.' – Amy

'Shoes absolutely have to be clean and neat, not scuffed up and dirty. Make an effort and clean then before you go out, and never, ever wear a Velcro fastening.' – Jessica

'Palmer's Cocoa Butter is the best moisturiser. It's pretty much all you need.' – Mark

'Spray tans aren't great for the guys. It's too much like putting on make-up.' – Arg

'Make-up isn't necessarily a no. You can finesse your look with a little foundation, bronzer and eyebrow pencil if necessary.' – Harry

'A lot of guys in Essex wear make-up. Clear mascara, bronzer, pressed powder. They just don't tell you. You see it in their drawers.' – Lydia

'Don't wear too many rips in your jeans. One or two is just enough. Be careful not to Essex it too much.' – Mark

'Mark's shaved his chest and I think it looks disgusting.' – Lucy

PROM NIGHT: A VERY ESSEX EVENING

Every Essex girl's life can be marked by a series of significant dresses but there are two that stand out more than any. Of course there's the wedding dress, but then there's what many consider the dress rehearsal: Prom Night.
  As part of her role at Forever Unique, Lucy helps would-be Prom Queens select their big dress time after time, so here are her tips on how to attend your prom in true Essex style.

- Colour is essential if you want to turn up in true red-carpet style, which *of course* you do – be bold and show off your tan in coral, aqua or hot pink.
- Choose between either prints (floral or stripe) or plain fabric with loads of bling accessories.
- Don't wear black. Never, ever wear black. Why would you do that to yourself?
- If you're going short, make sure it's fitted over the bust and then kicks out for a mini princess look. (Think Amy at Essex Fashion Week.)
- If you're going floor length, remember that you can take it up later and wear the frock again. No one will ever know!

- Whatever you do, avoid a hem that falls just above your ankle: it shortens your legs and makes you look mumsy.
- This season is all about 'casual Grecian': messy side buns and loose curls.
- Your body must be glossy and glowing but please: no Oompa Loompas. St Tropez shimmer stick will help you on your neckline and arms.
- If your dress has no glitz a crystal bling bag is a must – with matching shoes.
- And most importantly: no meringue dresses. You want to eat the dessert, not look like it.

THE HISTORY OF ESSEX –
THE ORANGE COUNTY

It wasn't always flash cars, deep tans and sausage plaits, you know. Essex has a long and illustrious history – which includes giving us some of our greatest national figures.

Kings and Queens of Essex

Denise Van Outen
This Basildon Blonde has gone from being a lads' mag favourite in the 1990s to an iconic showbiz figure and happily settled mum of one. She's still as proud as ever of her Essex roots and also has a totally hot husband.

Lady Mary Wroth
This Essex lady lived the good life in Loughton in the 1600s and made a name for herself with her wild antics. She kept her husband on rations until he died, snogged her married cousin and went on to have kids with him, then published poems and books about the escapades. Don't cross an Essex girl.

Helen Mirren
This sexy stunner who played the Queen of England to Oscar-winning perfection was raised east of Dagenham, but she was brought up in Westcliff-on-Sea and went to school in Southend. What do you mean you're surprised? All the clues are there – she's got great hair, great frocks and she's never afraid to speak her mind.
Of course she's from Essex.

Martina Cole
Born and raised in Aveley, Martina Cole has gone on to be an infamous chronicler of the seedier side of Essex. The feisty females in her novels seem rather familiar to anyone who has caught the sharp side of an Essex woman's tongue.

Stacey Solomon
Unheard of until 2009 and then forgotten by 2010, it looked as if the *X Factor* had both given and taken away Stacey's one chance at fame. But her appearance in the jungle in *I'm a Celebrity Get Me Out of Here* last year cemented her place in our hearts and now it looks as if the Dagenham Diva is here to stay.

Billy Bragg
Musician and left-wing activist Bragg might not share the politics of a lot of his county but he is still a Barking boy through and through. The grandson of a man who worked for a local hat and cap maker, he is now a celebrated voice on the radio for both his music and his opinions. He proves the diversity of the Essex man.

Fact:
The name Essex originates from the expression 'Land of the East Saxons'.

Fact:
In 1588 Queen Elizabeth 1 addressed the navy from Tilbury in Essex before they headed off for the Spanish invasion.

Fact:
in 1722 Daniel Defoe toured Essex and his account describes oyster fishing and game shooting on the marshes.

Fact:
Hylands Park, these days the location for V Festival, used to be a Prisoner of War camp.

Fact:
Chelmsford is referred to as the 'birthplace of radio' and on 15 June 1920 the Marconi wireless factory broadcast the first official sound broadcast in the UK.

Fact:
Tiptree in Essex is one of very few places in the world where the 'Little Scarlet' strawberry is commercially grown. It is Wilkin & Sons jam makers that grow the rare strawberries.

Jamie Oliver
This Essex prince has taken his countrymen's taste for home-cooked dinners and turned into an empire of epic proportions. He has sausage-plaited himself to multi-millionaire status and has the model wife and family to prove it. A hard-working Essex lad who has made his county proud.

Russell Brand
Born and raised in Grays, Essex nobleman Russell Brand is one of the county's most flamboyant exports, but he's still a devoted West Ham fan. Now a celebrated movie star living in Los Angeles with his pop megastar wife Katy Perry and her fabulous manicures, he truly is living the Essex dream.

Frank Lampard
Son of a West Ham player and assistant manager, Lampard attended Brentwood High School and has Essex running through him like a stick of rock. He may live in a Surrey mansion now but the Chelsea player is a shining example of an Essex man living his heritage loud and proud wherever he is.

Dermot O'Leary
The king of reality TV was born and raised in Colchester. His parents may be Irish but his attitude is all Essex. After humble beginnings at Radio Essex he went on to play a crucial role in T4, Big Brother and the X Factor. And all while rocking a snappy wardrobe.

LIFESTYLE

ESSEX À LA CARTE

Essex cuisine revolves around one thing: the perfect home-cooked dinner.

And as far as home-cooked dinners go, the absolute, definitive, and indisputable authority is Nanny Pat. She ran a pub for several years and was a school cook for 26 years, so she pretty much has a black belt in Sausage Plaiting. Nanny Pat will never part with the secret recipe for her sausage plait, so here is a classic recipe with a selection of her dos and don'ts...

Mark says:

'Sausage plaits are phenomenal.'

Nanny Pat says:

'Everything tastes excellent when someone else is cooking it.'

A CLASSIC SAUSAGE PLAIT

Ingredients

1 x 375g/13oz packet readymade puff pastry
1 tbsp butter
1 small onion, diced
1kg/2¼lb good sausage meat
1 free-range egg, beaten

Method

Preheat the oven to 200°C/400°F/Gas mark 6.

Roll out the pastry into a rectangle about 25cm/10in by 20cm/8in.

Heat the butter in a frying pan, and add the onion, cooking until it is softened but not coloured.

In a mixing bowl, combine the onion and the sausage meat well.

Put the sausage mixture down the middle of the long length of the pastry. With a sharp knife, cut slits 3cm/1in apart, 1cm/½in away from the sausage mixture to the edge of the pastry, slanting away from you. Brush with beaten egg.

Starting at the end nearest to you, fold the pastry alternately over each other, to give a 'plait' effect. Brush the top with beaten egg.

Transfer to a baking tray and bake in the centre of the oven for 40 minutes, reducing the temperature to 150°C/300°F/Gas mark 2 after 20 minutes. Serve in slices hot or cold.

DON'T

Get carried away with adding ingredients such as red peppers and mushrooms.

Worry about using egg or milk to brush the top of the finished plait. Either will do.

Disrespect the sausage plait. It is a thing of beauty.

DO

Bear in mind that you don't have to cook the onions first. You can just make sure that they are very very finely chopped.

Add extras such as thyme, garlic, mustard powder if that is to your taste.

Remember to keep it simple. The secret is simplicity every time.

THE PRIDE OF ESSEX

Something that Essex celebrates more than flash cars, big hair and sausage plaits, is being proud to be who you are. There are some who think of Essex as a place to be laughed at – but those who actually grew up there are proud of their birthplace. There's no point in having the best nails in the room if you've got the worst attitude...

- You can't change where you grew up, so make sure you're proud of it. Find out who grew up near you and what they went on to do, regardless of whether it made the papers or not.
- Get working on something to be proud of in the future too though – exams, career, following those showbiz dreams. Be the inspiration for the next generation!
- Don't try and change yourself for someone you fancy. You are you, and that is enough!
- Never forget that you don't have to be the same as everyone else – celebrate your individuality, whether you do it by what you wear, what you say or what you drive.

- Always turn up to a party prepared to be kind to someone else there – so much classier than causing a scene or a row. Behave as if the papers would be writing about you tomorrow, even if tomorrow finds you delivering the papers, rather than being in them.
- Looking good doesn't come without working hard, so if you want the lifestyle you've got to be prepared to put in the work, whether it's at a desk, a massage bed or a recording studio.

HARRY'S GUIDE TO COMING OUT

Harry feels very strongly about other teens not being as supported as he was when talking about their sexuality and who they really are...

'You should never ever have to hold your feelings in about who you are. Let it out!'

If you think you need someone to talk to and don't feel able to talk to any of your friends or family, you can call the charity Stonewall on 08000 502020 or visit their website at www.stonewall.org.uk. Good luck and stay proud!

THE ESSEX GUIDE TO WHEELS

In Essex, everyone drives everywhere. As Mark points out, 'If you don't drive, you don't get about.'

But it's not just about getting from A to B, it's about looking good and feeling great while doing it. The Essex way to drive involves showing off what you've got and making sure that you're as comfortable as possible when you're making that all important journey from the King William to Deuces. Turning up sweaty from the Tube or late because of the bus just isn't the Essex way.

Oh, and guys, don't think you can get one over on the girls here ... because Essex girls know their motors. Here's the guide to who drives what in *The Only Way is Essex*, what they wish they drove, and a few of their thoughts on the world of wheels.

Mark

ACTUALLY DRIVES: A White Mercedes
LONGS TO DRIVE: A Lamborghini. 'I had a model of it in my bedroom as a kid. I'll get it one day.'
WHAT DOES HE LOOK FOR IN A CAR?: Comfort and style
MOTORING PHILOSOPHY: 'In Essex you can look like **** but if you drive past in a nice car then the girls' heads will turn.'

Lauren

ACTUALLY DRIVES: A 4x4 Kia
LONGS TO DRIVE: A Bentley convertible
WHAT DOES SHE LOOK FOR IN A CAR?: 'It's all about what it says about you.'
MOTORING PHILOSOPHY: 'A smart car gives a guy status. I have to be with someone who has a bit of status, and if he's driving a really nice car, you know that he does.'

Harry

ACTUALLY DRIVES: Mostly he gets driven around in his mum's BMW.
LONGS TO DRIVE: A massive white Range Rover with leather seats and a crystal-encrusted steering wheel
WHAT DOES HE LOOK FOR IN A CAR?: A lift, until he passes his test…
MOTORING PHILOSOPHY: 'A vajazzled steering wheel would be amazing.'

Amy

ACTUALLY DRIVES: A CLC Kompressor in white
LONGS TO DRIVE: A white Range Rover with spinning rims.
WHAT DOES SHE LOOK FOR IN A CAR?: Spinning rims and hydraulics. 'I think that's more cool than anything on earth. In fact, *Pimp My Ride* is one of my favourite programmes'
MOTORING PHILOSOPHY: 'I can pull up in a nice car but it's not the be all and end all. Joe doesn't even drive at all.'

Jessica

ACTUALLY DRIVES: A Peugeot 206 cc convertible
LONGS TO DRIVE: A Mercedes SLK , Aston Martin DB5
WHAT DOES SHE LOOK FOR IN A CAR?: Something that looks good!
MOTORING PHILOSOPHY: 'If a guy's driving a nice car, it will make you find him more appealing, but that won't matter if he's an absolute idiot.'

Sam

ACTUALLY DRIVES: A black Mini
LONGS TO DRIVE: A series 1 convertible. Or maybe a pearlised Aston Martin with matching cream leather. 'Oh, and if I have any spare cash I might get a Rolls-Royce Phantom.'
WHAT DOES SHE LOOK FOR IN A CAR?: Speed, not comfort. 'I like a car with a large engine.'
MOTORING PHILOSOPHY: 'Guys – no Skodas and no estate cars. What are you doing? Who wants to be collected in a seven-seater?'

Lucy

ACTUALLY DRIVES: A black Mini with metallic stripes. It was bought at the same time as Sam's almost identical one.
LONGS TO DRIVE: The same mini but covered in Swarovski crystals. All over.

WHAT DOES SHE LOOK FOR IN A CAR?: Sparkles
MOTORING PHILOSOPHY: 'Maybe I shouldn't admit this but it does make a massive difference what car a guy comes to pick you up in.'

Arg

ACTUALLY DRIVES: He hasn't passed his test yet
LONGS TO DRIVE: Anything
WHAT DOES HE LOOK FOR IN A CAR?: Style and comfort
MOTORING PHILOSOPHY: 'Stay safe and look good.'

Lydia

ACTUALLY DRIVES: Did drive a Fiat 500 until it was written off recently.
LONGS TO DRIVE: A little vintage car
WHAT DOES SHE LOOK FOR IN A CAR?: Uniqueness
MOTORING PHILOSOPHY: 'I want them to see me coming'

Kirk

ACTUALLY DRIVES: A BMW CLK
LONGS TO DRIVE: A massive, classic, shiny Cadillac. Painted purple.
WHAT DOES HE LOOK FOR IN A CAR?: Comfort and style.
MOTORING PHILOSOPHY: 'You won't buy the most comfortable car in the world if it looks like a baked bean can.'

Nanny Pat

ACTUALLY DRIVES: Nanny Pat doesn't drive: she is driven
LONGS TO DRIVE: She doesn't long to drive. She was too busy to learn with 5 kids.
WHAT DOES SHE LOOK FOR IN A CAR?: A lift.
MOTORING PHILOSOPHY: Nanny Pat's happy to take the bus as it's good to walk a while. She even got away with forgetting her bus pass recently.

THE PETS OF ESSEX

In Essex, almost everything is big – big hair, big boobs, big cars. That's almost everything. Because having a pet the Essex way means having a micro-pet. What easier way to make your heels look higher or your chest look bigger than to be accompanied by a dog who is hardly bigger than a hot-water bottle? Well, either a dog or ... a pig.

The micro-pig

Thrilled that their love had been reignited, Arg surprised his girlfriend Lydia with a micro-pig as a Christmas gift this year. She had mentioned that she fancied one after seeing a magazine article about Victoria Beckham's micro-pigs, but she wasn't entirely prepared for the pig to arrive so immediately.

At first Lydia thought she would have to return it as rearing a pig seemed just too much responsibility…and the farmer came to collect him. But after chatting with him, Lydia realised she could never part with Mr Darcy. Once he had a name he was part of the family and soon everyone had fallen in love with him. Before long, Lydia had applied for her holding licence and walking licence for the local council and rural farm agency, and the pair of them were regularly taking strolls though Epping Forest together. (Micro-pigs are not allowed to walk down high streets or anywhere with fast-food outlets because of the risk of foot and mouth disease.)

These days, Mr Darcy has a huge blue thatched Wendy House at the end of Lydia's garden. It's filled with straw and a leather-and-fur bed, but he still likes to come into the house to show the couple some love when they're curled up watching TV. He's entirely house-trained, and is now one of the family. Love reigns!

Essex-ing up your pet

- The poodle parlour is a must. All little dogs love a wash and a bit of a massage.
- A Swarovski-studded collar is always a good idea. Lucy's dog Caspar has one.
- Matching coats are a good look. Amy is devastated that Pucci is now so fat that she can't get a coat on her!
- Halloween is a great time for Essex pets, as it's another opportunity to dress up your dogs. Amy took hers trick-or-treating last year.
- Painted toenails are for the truly devoted.

The micro-dog

It doesn't matter what breed of dog you have in Essex as long as it's tiny!

- Mark bought younger sister Natalia a sausage-dog puppy named Bubbles for Christmas. He's already a favourite of Nanny Pat and Jessica, despite needing to be lifted over the step out of the French windows every time he needs to go outside. Mark goes to visit him every day.
- Harry has a shih-tzu named Reggie, as his older brother is named Ronnie. He and his mum adore him and lavish affection on him.
- Sam's dog Ted is a chug, a chihuahua and pug cross.
- Amy has two dogs: Pucci is the fat, greedy pug with a black face and Pudgsly is the black one, who is more her mum's dog, really.
- Lauren wants to get a puppy but is hesitating as unlike the rest of the cast she doesn't live with family who could look after it when she's busy working.
- Kirk is the only one with pets bigger than a handbag. He has two rottweilers named Scrappy and Tia, a german shepherd named Kia and two racehorses named Kilkenny Bay and Monaco Dreams. Oh, and some chickens, and nine Koi Carp in his pond.
- Lucy has a little Westie called Caspar, as well as a cat called Cookie … and fish, rabbits and guinea pigs.

'No, we won't get more. One pig's enough.' – Arg

'Oh yeah, I might have to get him a Mrs Darcy.' – Lydia

MARBELLA: ESSEX ON SEA

The only place more Essex than Essex is Marbella. Favourite holiday destination (after Disneyland) for most of the cast, it's a home away from home for the TOWIE gang. Here is everything you ever need to know about the Costa del sol hotspot...

- Marbella only had 900 residents until 1946, when German Prince Maximilian de Hohenlohe-Langenburg and his son Alfonso were driving through the town and had a problem in their Rolls-Royce. They liked the area so much that they bought some land, built a house and sold plots to their mega-rich friends.
- Sam's family lived here twice, and she can speak Spanish as a result of her time at the Aloha International School.
- Joan Collins is said to have accepted her iconic role as Alexis Colby-Carrington in *Dynasty* from her villa in Marbella.
- Inspired by films like *Sexy Beast* and *The Business*, it's where the lads spend every May bank holiday on a boys' trip.
- Marbella has a Bonsai museum. Go figure.
- Arg and Lydia lived in Marbella last year, until their upsetting – but temporary – split.
- Marbella holds a 'patio contest' every year in May, when locals compete to see who has the most beautiful patio.
- Piers Morgan has called Marbella 'Butlins for Billionaires'.
- Marbella used to be a favourite destination for Hollywood icons Cary Grant, Audrey Hepburn and Sir Laurence Olivier.
- Most of the cast have some family living in Marbella.

HOLIDAY ESSENTIALS

- White bikini for showing off your tan – just make sure that it's a 'real' tan. No one wants to cover their sun lounger in streaky self-tanning lotion, and it's a shocking way to ruin a bikini.
- Neon bikini for showing off your tan – colour isn't so important but pink, orange and blue will all do nicely.
- Sunglasses – massive. It's the Essex spirit to behave like an international superstar even if you're only on a bank holiday break with a bunch of mates you grew up with. So think Lady Gaga meets defiant WAG. Sunnies on, chin up, greet your public.
- Kaftan – you know how everyone says they'll lose weight on holiday because it will just be fresh salads and local produce? That never happens. There is calamari. There are chips. There are cocktails by the pool. So there will be a least one day when you want a little something to give you some extra coverage.
- Sun block – sun beds are very, very bad for you. A little vitamin D from the natural sun is not nearly as bad. You still need to strike the delicate balance between having a spray tan the day before you fly and going home a similar, but natural, golden brown. To avoid two days indoors weeping at your glowing pink skin you need sun

block. Yes, it is boring. But it is essential. The Essex way around the tedium is to have as much fun as possibly applying it. You see, *now* it seems fun…

- Heeled beach shoes – flip-flops may be practical, and they're undeniably comfortable. But they don't give a girl the wiggle she deserves. You need to find a nice heeled wedge, or a cute sandal for your poolside strut. But beware – a wedge does not work in sand. It is *far* from a good look.
- Floppy-brimmed hat – you might not think you need one but we have one word for you: hangovers. That is all.
- Gossip magazines – when you're at the airport is seems as if you've bought too many. But there is never too many. Get as many as you can carry, because idly flicking through photographs of soap stars struggling with the rain in a pair of tatty Primark joggers is what sun loungers were made for.
- Insect spray – it stinks. But the only thing worse than smelling of mosquito repellant is when they bite you on the face and you have to spend the rest of the holiday explaining to people that you're not a pizza face, you're just tasty to mozzies.
- Lip gloss – always lip gloss. Nothing is anything without lip gloss.

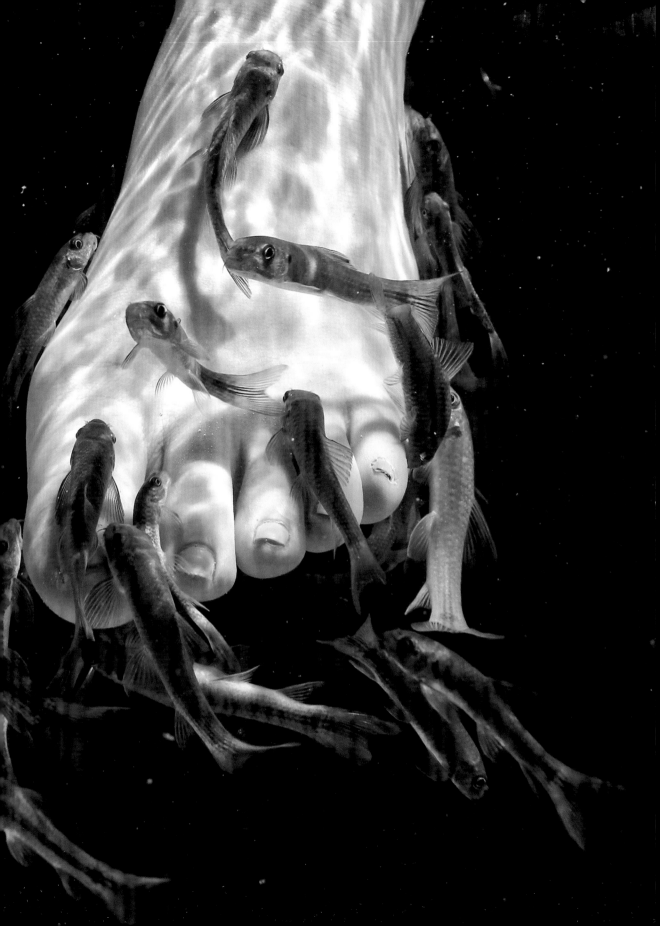

WORLD OF INTERIORS

There's no point in looking Essex if your house doesn't. And the same goes for your office or our next nightclub. The rules are simple.

- Comfort comes first. The bigger the better.
- If it can be bought in purple, buy it in purple.
- If it can't be bought in purple, buy it in black leather.
- If it can't be bought in black leather, get the most expensive one and cover it in Swarovski crystals.
- Then get a tiny version of it for your dog.

- Bleached wood is the finest of the woods. Use wherever possible.
- No need for an ironing board. Your kitchen island will do.
- If in doubt, scatter a few animal print cushions around.
- Make sure that your TV is as big as your wall will support.
- Don't forget – these rules also apply to the micro-pig's Wendy house.

IF ESSEX RULED THE WORLD

There are global problems, and there are Essex problems, but what happens when you bring the two together? We think today's world leaders could do worse than listen to the logic of the *TOWIE* cast because, lets face it, Essex is most definitely a glass half full kind of place!

'It's hard to care about global warming when you've lived through a war.' –Nanny Pat

'I don't think we should think about the banking crisis. You've got to look on the bright side a bit more. We're all so depressed we're just making it worse.' – Amy

'Putting up tuition fees is terrible. If people want to study to make their lives better they should be able to.' – Harry

'Global warming would be brilliant. It would be hot every day and everyone would sit around tanned looking amazing in bikinis.' – Mark

'You should be able to go to university on merit as opposed to how much money your family's got.' – Arg

'People can work to support themselves too though. I went to McDonalds and the guy in there had such a posh voice. So I asked what he was doing in there and he said he was saving because he was at Oxford and Cambridge.' – Amy

'To solve the recession I reckon upping wages, changing all the buses to limos and free spray tans for all would cheer everyone up.' – Sam

'Middle-East crisis? No problem. I'd take them all down to Deuces and it would all be sweet.' – Mark

'People need to relax, stop panicking and save their money as well as just spunking it. The recession will pass by eventually.' – Arg

CAREERS

ESSEX SCHOOLDAYS

Aaaah, schooldays. Whether you spend them knuckling down to work or staring out the window, dreaming of Friday night, they can be the best – and worst – days of your life. Our cast may not have been the most committed pupils in the world – they were much too busy 'exercising independent fashion decisions' or bunking off to spend time with their mates for that – but they do have some tips and tricks for getting through school the Essex way.

- Do not let bullying be any part of your life. There's no excuse for bullying and you should never be afraid to tell someone if you are being bullied. Celebrate who you are, know your true friends, and never let any problem get out of hand because you are too afraid to talk about it.
- Remember – if you don't show up at class and then tweet about the great day you had down the high street, the chances are you will be caught.
- 'Voulez vous couchez avec moi' may sound impressive when you hear it on the radio, but it's best not to say that to someone in any position of authority.

- No one wants you to go to school because they don't like you. They just want you to learn enough so that you can go on to do the kind of job you want to. Make the most of not having to worry about paying bills.
- It may only be school but that's no reason not to devote adequate time and attention to your look. Take Harry and Amy's lead on the fashion front, but maybe try to make it to classes on time as well.
- It's not just make-up that you can experiment with – make sure you personalise your uniform too. Skirt length needs to be perfect, collar needs to be popped, socks need to be down.

- Girls: beware boys who call themselves 'The Inbetweeners'. Boys: avoid girls who call themselves 'The Plastics'.
- Never say that the dog ate your homework. Dogs the size of handbags could barely manage to keep down a stamp let alone a notebook.
- Try your very, very hardest not to be disappointed if every day isn't like Glee. But remember, Essex it up and it could feel like Glee.
- Don't forget an apple for teacher every now and again. The old Essex charm goes a long, long way...

THE WORLD OF LOLA – HOW TO BE A POP STAR

Standing for Loveable Outrageous Loud Ambitious, LOLA were originally formed by Lindsay a couple of years ago. Since Christmas LOLA has been comprised of Amba, Jessica, Lauren and Megan. A modern-day Spice Girls they are full of sparkle, sass and sexiness.

Lola have done things the hard way – finding the right management, vocal training, rehearsing routines. Here are our top tips on getting a little pop star into your life.

- Never show up first to an event. You want to make sure everyone is in a panic that you might be a no-show before you're caught within 100 metres of the entrance.
- Learn how to get out of a car with dignity. Knees together, then turn. Never, ever, let one leg out first. Flashing your smalls is a fast route to either the tabloids or Twitter, it's your *face* you want people to recognise.
- Turn up with security. And if you can't afford security make sure you've got a mate or a big brother on hand to usher you in and out of the cold.
- Never ask for a goodie bag. It is the fastest way to show yourself up if you're at an event with freebies. Look as if you're only accepting it to be polite. Then spend the taxi ride home checking out what you've got.
- Don't have an uncool rider. Weird eating habits are very old school. Just ask for candles and water. And if you don't have a rider, this also applies to staying over at your boyfriends'. No one likes a picky eater but everyone likes a beautifully scented room.

- Be charming to your entourage. Remember: make-up artists hear everything. And they don't forget it. They tell other make-up artists... word gets round. And if you don't have a fleet of make-up artists, just make sure you tip your hairdresser so they don't skimp on colour.
- Lock your phone. Everyone's lost their phone at some stage. If it's locked, your biggest worry is a tedious call to your insurance company. If it's unlocked, you may find you have lifted the lid on top secret gossip.
- Never try and keep anything you were only supposed to be trying on. No one wants to get busted 'Doing a Lohan'.
- Don't lose too much weight. Those gasps you hear when you unveil your outfit should be envy, not concern.
- Keep something back. Go on, just a little something.

HOW ESSEX ARE YOU?

Think you know your Fake Bake from your fake Burberry? You might have the tan, the heels and wheels, but you'll never be truly Essex until you can answer all of these questions. Are you a wannabe or a true *TOWIE* fan?

1   What's the name of Amy's mum and who is her sister?

2   How white did Sam want her teeth bleached?

3   You're a bloke. You want a Vajazzle. But what do you ask for in the salon?

4   Can you remember the name of the girl that Arg tried to chat up on the speed-dating night?

5   What is the best thing to polish glass with, if you do things the Nanny Pat way?

6   What was Julian's nickname for the LOLA girls?

7   How did Kirk train for the big fight while Mark had Arg cycling along beside him?

8   Which hospital were both Mark and Lauren born in?

9   What was the job that Kirk hated more than any other before working at Sugar Hut?

10   Which bar would you go to for an Essex speed-dating event?

11   What does the tattoo on Kirk's chest say?

12   Who got Arg into singing in restaurants, kick-starting his career?

13   Who did Lauren and Mark pose as for Now magazine?

14   What date was the series first aired on ITV2?

15   What to Maria Fowler is the male
      equivalent of being on Page 3?

16   Who does Lydia compare Arg to when she catches
      him auditioning girls for the boxing match?

17   Where do they love hip hop, according to
      Lauren 'Popey' Pope?

18   What sticky fruit does Harry
      say he feels like after his spray tan?

19   Who was voted the most popular cast member?

20   What is the only way?

Are you in the know, or just
a well jel wannabe?

Answers on page 134

FITNESS

WORKING OUT

There's no point in having the hair and nails if you don't have the beautiful body to match. And that takes hard work and dedication. But don't despair – working out the Essex way needn't mean hours spent alone sweating on a treadmill. In Essex, fitness is just another excuse for socialising and looking good. Here are our Dos and Don'ts for working out the Essex way.

DO

- Keep it social. Lucy is a huge fan of hip-hop/Latin exercise craze Zumba, because it feels like being at a party and leaves you looking like Shakira. Lauren is also a fan.

- Remember that dancing is a good fitness alternative. Both Jessica and Harry find that the constant dance rehearsals that are such an important part of their showbiz lifestyle are their main source of fitness.

- If you struggle to concentrate in the gym, give something more intense like boot camp a go. Amy spent time in January at a fitness boot camp and loved every minute, even the immense pizza cravings.

- Make the most of your time on the cross trainer. As Sam points out, it is multi-purpose: 'If you're in a tight top on the cross trainer, it's going to draw attention no matter what. Use that – and then ignore him.'

- Turn up looking the part. Amy recommends that the best gym look is 'a nice pair of leggings, a matching top, hair up in a bun and a slick of make-up.'

What the cast say...

'I'm not going to lie to you, I do put on a bit of make-up.' – Amy

'Reebok EasyTone trainers have a little bit of a heel to make your legs look longer.' – Sam

'At the end of the day, if you see a good-looking guy in the gym, you're not going to not have a look.' – Amy

✗ DON'T

- Be afraid of wearing make-up to the gym. Sam recommends 'a base, a bit of bronzer and a bit of lippy. You don't want to look like you're trying too hard but of course you want to look pretty.'

- Forget that everyone needs a little vitamin D after exercise. Mark likes to achieve this by having a 'bit of a wander around to the outdoor pool. Nothing to do with checking out what the girls are wearing though'.

- Be anything less than 100% confident in the gym. You're there to make yourself feel good and look good.

- Ever end a workout without a proper stretch. As Sam points out 'Stretching is the most eye-catching exercise of all.'

ESSEX FITNESS ALTERNATIVES: PING-PONG AND THE SPLITS

It doesn't all have to be personal trainers and treadmills. If there's anything Essex is keen to celebrate, it's doing things your own way. So for those who find the gym just that little bit too boring – here are some Essex alternatives.

The splits

'Once you can do the splits, it's a gift for life. Everyone will be impressed when you drop to the dance floor.' – Harry

All-singing, all-dancing, Harry Derbridge decided that he wanted to be able to do the splits when he was the tender age of six. By nine years old he had achieved his goal and could at last 'whack 'em out'. He suggests that it is a minimum of two years of hard work for anyone hoping to achieve the same mighty goal, and here's his step-by-step guide:

1. Find a room with a ballet bar in. Or perhaps just a room with a sofa that you can use instead
2. Put one leg up on the ballet bar/back of the sofa, and push that raised leg further away from you along the bar
3. Respect gravity. Do not attempt to do the splits in a horizontal position until you can do them standing at the bar/sofa.

And remember – it's not easy. You will have to watch many episodes of *Keeping Up with the Kardashians* with one leg raised before you can reach the dream. But take these words as your guiding light:

'You have to work hard for the things that you really want. And I really wanted to be able to do the splits. So I had to work hard.' – Harry

Ping-pong

'I am a professional ping pong player. I absolutely love it.' – Amy

Amy Childs is more than just a pretty face. She was also a child prodigy. After seeing a game of ping-pong that some other children were playing, Amy and her brother asked for lessons. The fact that ping-pong originated as an after dinner parlour game for toffs in the 1880s didn't put her off. And nor did the fact that it used to be called 'wiff-waff'.

Before long, a star was born. Amy's skill and ease with a bat and ball was quickly revealed. Soon she was a member of her local club and shortly after that she was playing for Essex. She travelled all around the country representing her county, until she gave it up as a teenager when the attractions of boys and strip lashes took over. This is a real shame, as in 1988 Table Tennis was made an Olympic sport. We live in hope. And if you want to carry on where Amy left off, here's how…

1. You can find your local club at www.englishtabletennis.org.uk or, if you're in Essex: www.essextabletennis.org.uk
2. Get all the kit you need at www.tabletennispro.co.uk
3. Back straight, eyes focused, don't let your enemy take you by surprise – you are now ready to play ping-pong. Long may you loop, flip and smash.

'When I see a table in a pub I am still itching to have a go.' – Amy

THE A–Z OF ESSEX

A ASTON MARTIN – dream car for most Essex girls

B BONGOS – Kirk's hidden talent is that he can play them

C CHUGS – the chihuahua-pug cross is the ultimate Essex Pet

D DUBAI – where the Ryans tried to persuade Lauren to follow them for work. Did she go?

E EASTENDERS – the soap of choice for the Essex birds and blokes

F FALSIES – lashes, boobs, hair…

G GIRL POWER – all the girls were into the Spice Girls as kids

H HAIR EXTENSIONS – without them, the Essex economy would collapse

I IRONING – nobody panic, Nanny Pat's got it under control

J JUMPERS – essential festive wear for Mark and Arg

K KEEN – never, ever seem to be keen in Essex

L LORD OF PARLIAMENT – the man Amy thinks is in charge of the country

M MR DARCY – not a literary hero, but Lydia's romantic festive gift from Arg

N NATURAL LOOK – never seen in Essex

O OH MY GOD!!

P PEARLISED – all the best things are pearlised in Essex. Cars, phones, lip glosses

Q QUEEN OF ESSEX – voiceover star Denise van Outen, of course

R ROSÉ – the wine of choice for the ladies of Essex. Unless there's champagne around

S SWAROVSKI – essential Essex accessory

T THE RISING SUN – the name of the East End pub that Nanny Pat and her husband used to run

U 'UMBRELLA' – by the beautiful songstress Rihanna, Essex's favourite singer

V If you thought this one would be anything other than VAJAZZLE, you'll never be allowed to cross the Essex county barrier again

W WORK – not, as in hard graft, but as in 'that's a lot of work…'

X X-RAY VISION – to see what's under the layers of bling and tan

Y YOUR PLACE OR MINE? – no cheesy chat-up lines please

Z ZOO – Well, Kirk got a snog out of it, didn't he?

CONCISE ESSEX ENGLISH DICTIONARY

A glossary of terms to help you speak like a native and make yourself heard on Loughton High Road!

Aren't I?:
Rhetorical question to be added to the end of statements, creating emphasis by asking a question that does not need to be answered. E.g. 'I'm organising Essex Fashion week, aren't I?'

Babe:
What you call your girlfriend when you're trying to calm her down or persuade her of something. E.g. 'Of course I still see my ex, babe, she goes to my gym the whole time.'

Beautiful:
'That's a good idea.' Adjective to describe anything or any situation that is in any way positive.

Chug:
A blend of the chihuahua and pug dog. Also know as a chughuahua.

Cotching:
'We're just cotching.' Relaxing, chilling.

Essex you up:
I am going to make you wear a pink shirt and put a lot of product in your hair now. E.g. 'Come over here, I'm going to Essex you right up before we meet the girls.'

Going for a bed:
'I am going to the gym or to the beauty salon to have a session on a sun bed now.'

Golden:
Good, pleasing. Like the very rays of the sun itself.

Haven't I?:
See 'AREN'T I'. N.B. an unfortunate consequence of these turns of phrase is that it can create the effect that you don't know where you are going or what you are doing at all.

How Funny:
'Brilliant, we've done this conversation. Let's move on to the next topic now.' Often used without a hint of laughter.

Idiot:
Mug, plank, plum.

Jel:
Jealous.

Malt:
An attractive woman. E.g. 'Cor, look at that malt at the bar.'

Minging:
Unattractive. So unappealing that you should probably be ashamed.

Mug:
Idiot, plank, plum

OMG:
Oh My God. Well I never!

Plank:
Idiot, mug, plum.

Plum:
Idiot, mug, plank.

Sort:
Attractive person, if perhaps a little naughty, member of the opposite sex. 'He's a sort, that one from the gym'

Shuuutup!:
'That gossip is so exciting that I can barely take it anymore! Stop! Be quiet or I shall explode!'

Share me some love:
'Please display some affection towards me.'

Slated:
'That did not go well.' Dissed, coated off.

Talk to me:
'Let's chat.'

Weapon:
An incredibly attractive woman.
E.g. 'She's a weapon.'

Well jel:
Really very jealous indeed.

100%:
Yes.

Concise
Essex English
Dictionary

ESSEX ONLINE: YOUR GUIDE TO THE BEST OF ESSEX ON THE INTERNET

Crystal Lounge: An Essex favourite
www.crystallounge.co.uk

Faces: So many nights, so little time…
www.facesnightclub.co.uk

Forever Unique: Where Lucy works,
where Lauren avoids…
www.foreverunique.co.uk

King William: The king of bars
www.thekingwilliamiv.co.uk -

Nu Bar: As they say, it's out with the old,
in the with the Nu
www.nubar.co.uk

Sugar Hut: It's not a nightclub,
it's a world
www.sugarhutworld.com

Vajazzles: Everything you need for a DIY
vajazzle night
www.vajazzle.me.uk

www.facebook.com/theonlywayisessex

www.itv.com/essex

TOWIE Twitter handles

@onlywayisessex
@_foreverunique
@harryderbidge
@JessWright_Lola
@kirk_offical
@LaurenGoodger
@LaurenPope
@lolaofficial_
@lucy_meck
@LydiaRoseBright
@MariaFowler
@MarkWright_
@MissAmyChilds
@OnlyWayIsEssex
@RealJamesArgent
@SamanthaFaiers

HOW ESSEX ARE YOU? QUIZ ANSWERS

Answers

1   Julie, and she's Harry's mum's sister
2   As white as Melinda Messenger's
3   A pejazzle
4   Chantelle
5   Vinegar and Water
6   'Pussycat Dolls'
7   He chased chickens around their coop in his garden
8   Whipps Cross
9   Being a welder
10 Cocktails & Dreams
11 Norcross
12 Lydia's mum
13 Prince William and Kate Middleton
14 10 October 2010
15 Playing for Chelsea
16 Hugh Hefner
17 China
18 An orange, duh
19 Amy Childs
20 Essex

Under 5 correct answers: O.M.G you'd better get reading up!
Better luck next time.
Between 5 – 10 correct answers: Someone hasn't been doing their homework, you're as naughty as our very own Mr.Wright.
Between 10 – 15 correct answers: Ok, we'll admit, you DO know your stuff – but practise makes perfect!
Over 15 correct answers: You're as Essex as a stick of Southend rock, congratulations, Nanny Pat would be proud!

ACKNOWLEDGEMENTS

The publishers would like to thank the cast of *The Only Way is Essex*
for their contributions to the book, and Alexandra Heminsley and the team at
Envy Design for bringing it all together so superbly. Also, many thanks to
Sean Marley and everyone at Lime Pictures Ltd, and ITV.

PHOTO CREDITS

With thanks to ITV plc, Getty Images and Corbis Images for supplying images
for this book. Kind thanks also to Owen Pouncy for supplying images
photographed for Forever Unique.